dress
smart

dress smart

a guide to effective personal packaging

SECOND EDITION

ANNE FENNER AND SANDI BRUNS

illustrations by sandi bruns

FAIRCHILD PUBLICATIONS, INC.
new york

This book is dedicated to our many friends who gave ideas, support, time, and testing to this project; to all persons who are growing to be themselves and to thousands of smart women and men who benefited from our first edition and taught us to make this one even better.

Executive Editor: Olga T. Kontzias
Art Director: Adam B. Bohannon
Director of Production: Priscilla Taguer
Associate Production Editor: Beth Applebome
Assistant Editor: Suzette Lam
Copy Editor: Barbara A. Chernow
Interior Design: Andrew Katz
Cover Design: Adam B. Bohannon

Second Edition, Copyright © 2004
Fairchild Publications, Inc.

First Edition, Copyright © 1988
Fairchild Publications, a division of Capital Cities Media, Inc.

Library of Congress Catalog Card Number: 2004101069

ISBN: 1-56367-316-9

GST R 133004424

Printed in the United States of America

contents

Women, begin with a questionnaire and move toward long-term wardrobe building. This chapter includes questions on image and style, body assets and figure faults, color, lifestyle, wardrobe, and clothing values. Who are you? Where are you going? What is your vision?

Men, begin with your own questionnaire. Discover the keys to building your best authentic look.

Who sees you? What do they see? Package yourself for great impact! Use written exercises, charts, illustrations, and diagrams to determine your marketing strategy. You never get a second chance at a first impression.

Project your individual style. Individual style can change and develop. This chapter analyzes the image and style sections of the questionnaire using written exercises, charts, illustrations, and diagrams. Style grows better with age.

Accentuate your assets and become aware of proportion and fit. This chapter uses graphics and written exercises to analyze the body asset and fault features of the questionnaire. If you stand in awe of the immensity of the sea and the beauty of flowers, you must also admire your body.

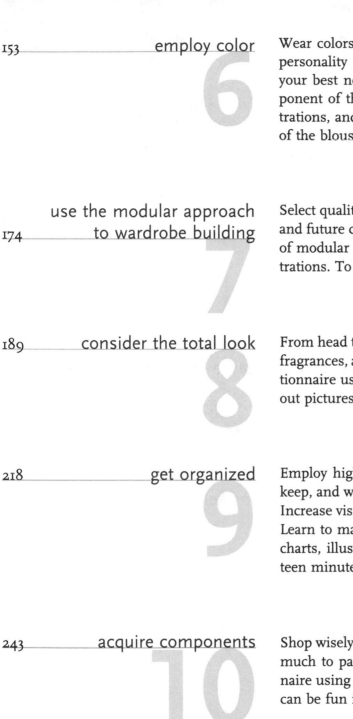

Wear colors that work for you. Consider your body pigmentation, personality type, and figure. Take into account your preferences, your best neutrals and colors' messages. Interpret the color component of the questionnaire, using written exercises, charts, illustrations, and diagrams. The face is often greener on the other side of the blouse!

Select quality not quantity, natural fibers, double-duty components, and future classics for your evolving way of life. Learn the principal of modular wardrobe building through exercises, charts, and illustrations. To simplify your life is a modern goal.

From head to toe, examine all dimensions. Learn about accessories, fragrances, and coordination. Analyze the wardrobe part of the questionnaire using written exercises and charts. Imagine a room without pictures or lamps. That's you with no finishing touches.

Employ high tech in your closet. Decide what to discard, what to keep, and what to alter. Combine and wear your clothing creatively. Increase visibility and accessibility by using your closet to its fullest. Learn to make your closet work for you through written exercises, charts, illustrations, and diagrams. You can dress in less than fifteen minutes when your closet is organized.

Shop wisely and well. Know what you need, where to look, and how much to pay. Analyze the clothing values section of the questionnaire using exercises, charts, illustrations, and diagrams. Shopping can be fun if you have a plan.

preface

You never get a second chance at a first impression.
—Will Rogers

At last! A fun, simple, step-by-step workbook to help you look and dress your best; a book that will become your very own because you will help write it. Here you will discover the looks that suit you and how to suit yourself accordingly—quickly and efficiently, with flair and style!

Remember, your clothing sends a primary visual message about you that no one can ignore, not even you! It is the packaging part of your marketing plan. Your clothing should be as terrific as your product, YOU. In fact, great packaging has been known to make a good product even better!

It's true! The smarter you dress, the smarter you look and the smarter you feel. Isn't it time for you to DRESS SMART? This revised *Dress Smart* is gender inclusive. Please do not read only the gender-specific sections (marked ♀ for women and ♂ for men). If a section is not marked for the opposite sex it is for you.

acknowledgments

Special thank you's to our families: Mike, Hilary, and Ben Fenner; Bill, Alyson, and Sarah Bruns; to our colleagues who originally helped formulate the first edition of *Dress Smart:* Dr. Gary Thibodeau, Mary Byington, Dr. Betty Tweeten, Bob Manders, Marilyn Homberg, Paula Cellar, Patricia Tuttle, Dr. Linda Alexander, and Kerstin VanDervoort; and to our willing subjects: Catherine Ferguson, Susan Cleary Johnson, Connie Spellman, Fran Teply, Bonnie Douglas, Alice Morton, Chris Hammans; Annette and Severin Huff, Wanda and Jennifer Gottschalk, Tina and Katie Broekemeier, Sandee Ourada, and the Junior League of Omaha Class Participants.

Camille Aponte at Katherine Gibbs School, the reviewer selected by the publisher, was also helpful in revising this book. And thank you to the many clients and associates over the past twenty years who continue to help us get smart.

Anne Fenner
Sandi Bruns

♀ gather data: women

1

Who are you, and what image do you project? What are your body's assets? What is important to you? What colors work for you? What do you wear, and where do you go? To define the direction your wardrobe should take, you need to take time to study *yourself*. Do not spend a lot of time on this questionnaire. Write down the first thing that comes to your mind. And have fun! We will get analytical later.

♀ evolutionize your look

1. Where are you now in your life/career? List five activities in which you presently participate.

a. _____

b. _____

c. _____

d. _____

e. _____

Who is the you in your future?

2. Who is the you in your future? Think of options! Remember your choices are wide open! In five or ten years you may be doing something you have not even heard of today. List what you expect your activities will be in five years.

a. _____

b. _____

c. _____

d. _____

e. _____

In ten years

a. _____

b. _____

c. _____

d. _____

e. _____

3. ▸ *Place an "X" in front of the wardrobe styles that best describe you now.*

  ▸ *Go back and circle the letters indicating the styles you want to enhance.*

_____ a. sophisticated	_____ j. severe
_____ b. romantic	_____ k. individualistic
_____ c. sensuous	_____ l. casual, sporty
_____ d. preppy	_____ m. earthy
_____ e. tailored	_____ n. smart, but not trendy
_____ f. dramatic	_____ o. classic, with flair
_____ g. understated quality,	_____ p. tweedy
_____ h. regal	_____ q. clothing as art
_____ i. authoritative	_____ r. international, ethnic

_____ s. neutral and natural   _____ w. "my only limitation is my imagination"

_____ t. clean and simple   _____ x. Western

_____ u. conservative   _____ y. sleek

_____ v. elegant   _____ z. other (please specify)

_____

4. ▶ *Place an "X" in front of the key words that describe your current image.*
   ▶ *Go back and circle the letters indicating the image you want to project in the future.*

_____ a. dramatic   _____ n. comfortable

_____ b. fashionable   _____ o. detailed, accessorized, finished

_____ c. confident   _____ p. matching, coordinated

_____ d. stylish   _____ q. colorful

_____ e. at ease   _____ r. unusual, unique

_____ f. energetic   _____ s. professional

_____ g. enthusiastic   _____ t. dainty

_____ h. robust   _____ u. perky, fresh

_____ i. determined   _____ v. inattentive to detail

_____ j. feminine   _____ w. couldn't care less about clothes

_____ k. successful   _____ x. careless

_____ l. tasteful   _____ y. carefree

_____ m. crisp and clean   _____ z. other (please specify)

_____

5. *Place an "X" in front of the statement that comes closest to describing your appearance.*

_____ a. Tall, high-fashion figure, extreme hair style, angular, striking features

_____ b. Strong, athletic build, casual and simple hair style, straight heavy brows, square shoulders, square jawline, informal casual manner

_____ c. Classic regular features, dignity combined with feminine charm, poised, gracious, and serene manner

_____ d. Beautiful figure, large eyes, glossy hair, rich coloring of hair and eyes, fair skin, beautiful features, sophisticated femininity

_____ e. Youthful appearance with carefree windblown hair, freckles, turned-up nose, friendly, casual manner, "little-boy look"

_____ f. Pretty, young looking, with softly curling hair, slightly tilted nose, dimpled and rounded checks, gently rounded figure, dainty and demure or gay and provocative

6. Place an "X" in front of the group of persons who seem most like you.

_____ a. Lauren Bacall, Barbra Streisand, Liza Minnelli, Diana Ross, Cher, Tina Turner, Greta Garbo, Brooke Shields, Indira Gandhi, Andrea Jung, Maya Angelou

_____ b. Ingrid Bergman, Candice Bergen, Ali MacGraw, Hillary Clinton, Carol Burnett, Diane Keaton, Jane Fonda, Venus Williams, Jamie Lee Curtis, Martha Stewart, Janet Reno, Margaret Thatcher

_____ c. Katharine Hepburn, Grace Kelly, Julie Andrews, Jane Pauley, Diane Sawyer, Diahann Carroll, Gwyneth Paltrow, Jackie Kennedy Onassis, Sandra Day O'Connor, Carly Fiorina, Condoleezza Rice

_____ d. Elizabeth Taylor, Zsa Zsa Gabor, Marilyn Monroe, Michelle Pfeiffer, Kim Basinger, Dolly Parton, Beverly Sills, Jennifer Lopez, Alice Walker, Oprah Winfrey, the Ahn Trio

_____ e. Leslie Caron, Goldie Hawn, Mary Martin, Annette Benning, Sarah Jessica Parker, Shirley Maclaine, Katie Couric

_____ f. Debbie Reynolds, Sandra Dee, Hayley Mills, Sally Struthers, Shirley Jones, Laura Bush, Alison Krauss, Britney Spears

7. *Place an "X" in front of the type of eyes that best describe yours.*

_____ a. Deep-set, heavy lids, close together, angled or slanted, direct gaze

_____ b. Average size, friendly, approachable

_____ c. Average size, clear, direct gaze

_____ d. Large, beautiful, melting, long lashed, alluring glance

_____ e. Wide open, wide apart, twinkling, friendly

_____ f. Large, round, wide open, long lashes, coy or demure glance

8. *Place an "X" in front of the type of build that best describes yours. Don't worry about weight or age.*

_____ a. Current fashion figure, angular, large boned, long legged

_____ b. Strong, muscular, sturdy, stocky, broad or square shoulders

_____ c. Average for height, well proportioned

_____ d. Feminine figure, long legged

_____ e. Small boned, compact, well coordinated

_____ f. Small boned, dainty, feminine, delicate

9. *Place an "X" in front of the type of posture that best describes yours.*

_____ a. Fashionable or erect, stiff, elevated chin, weight on heels

_____ b. Relaxed and casual, or vigorous and alert; solid, flat heeled, hands on hips

_____ c. Easily erect, poised, well balanced

_____ d. Graceful, willowy, relaxed

_____ e. Alert, perky, hands on hips

_____ f. Graceful, ballet posture, head tilted, appealing, compliant

10. *Place an "X" in front of the type of expressive manner that best describes yours.*

_____ a. Formal, dignified, reserved, haughty, sophisticated

_____ b. Free, easy, frank, open, friendly

_____ c. Gracious, poised, well mannered, mature, conventional, conservative, professional

_____ d. Flirtatious, charmingly feminine

_____ e. Direct, natural, "tomboy"

_____ f. Sparkling and gay, or demure and shy

11. *Place an "X" in front of the type of walk and gestures that best describe yours.*

_____ a. Decisive and energetic, or slow and purposeful

_____ b. Long strides, free swinging, large, easy, relaxed, natural

_____ c. Calm, poised, well controlled

_____ d. Graceful, languorous

_____ e. Quick, "skipping," free swinging, natural

_____ f. Graceful, dancing, light, airy

k. one shoulder higher than the other

l. high waist

m. long waist

n. protruding tummy

o. large derrière

p. unsure

q. none of the above

r. other (please specify)

_____

♀ enrich your raw materials

▸ *In questions 17–36, place an "X" to the left of the body characteristics that best describe you.*

▸ *Go back and circle the letter that indicates what you consider ideal.*

17. Body Size

_____ a. slender

_____ b. average

_____ c. plump

_____ d. big

18. Height

_____ a. short

_____ b. average

_____ c. tall

19. Foot Shape

_____ a. narrow

_____ b. average

_____ c. wide

20. Leg Shape

_____ a. slender

_____ b. average

_____ c. full

21. Leg Length

_____ a. short

_____ b. medium

_____ c. long

22. Derrière Shape

_____ a. flat

_____ b. rounded

_____ c. protruding

23. Hip Size

_____ a. narrow

_____ b. medium

_____ c. wide

24. Stomach

_____ a. flat

_____ b. rounded

_____ c. protruding

25. Waist Size

_____ a. small

_____ b. medium

_____ c. large

26. Hand Size

_____ a. small

_____ b. medium

_____ c. large

27. Arm Length

_____ a. short

_____ b. medium

_____ c. long

28. Arm Size

_____ a. thin

_____ b. average

_____ c. full

29. Bust or Chest Size

_____ a. small

_____ b. medium

_____ c. large

_____ d. extra large

30. Shoulders

_____ a. narrow

_____ b. average

_____ c. broad or square

_____ d. rounded or sloping

31. Neck

_____ a. short

_____ b. average

_____ c. long

_____ d. narrow

_____ e. broad

32. Teeth

_____ a. dull, yellowish

_____ b. white

_____ c. shiny, pearly

33. Lips

_____ a. thin

_____ b. medium

_____ c. thick

34. Nose Shape

_____ a. flat

_____ b. turned up

_____ c. pug

_____ d. hooked

_____ e. narrow

_____ f. wide

_____ g. straight

_____ h. long

_____ i. bumpy

35. Eye Size

_____ a. small

_____ b. medium

_____ c. large

36. Hair Type

_____ a. straight

_____ b. wavy

_____ c. curly

_____ d. kinky

37. Do you want to look

a. older

b. younger

c. taller

d. thinner

e. shorter

f. heavier

g. yourself

h. other (please specify)

_____

38. List your body assets.

_____

_____

_____

39. List your body challenges.

_____

_____

_____

♀ employ color

The correct colors are extremely important to any wardrobe. Each individual has certain colors that work best on her. The following questions are designed to help determine how you can use color to your best advantage. In response to questions 40–55, circle the letter for the answer that pertains to you.

♀ eye color

40. What is the color of your eyes? In bright daylight, study your eyes in a mirror and describe the colors and patterns that you observe. (You might want help from a friend on this one.)

_____

_____

_____

_____

_____

♀ hair color

41. What is the natural color of your hair?

a. blonde   d. gray

b. brown   e. black

c. red   f. other (please specify)

                              _____

42. If you are a natural blonde, is your natural hair color

a. ash blonde   e. flaxen blonde

b. "mousey" blonde   f. strawberry blonde

c. golden blonde   g. dark blonde

d. platinum blonde   h. other (please specify)

                              _____

43. If you have naturally brown hair, is it

a. golden   f. medium

b. chestnut   g. dark brown

c. red brown   h. taupe

d. "mousey"   i. other (please specify)

e. ash   _____

What is the natural color of your hair?

44. If your hair is naturally gray, would you describe it as

a. silver gray

d. golden gray

b. salt and pepper

e. premature

c. blue gray

f. other (please specify)

_____

45. If your hair is naturally black, would you describe it as

a. red black

b. blue black

c. brown black

d. ebony

e. salt and pepper

f. other (please specify) _____

46. If you have red in your hair, which of the following best describes it?

a. red highlights in medium brown hair

b. auburn

c. strawberry blonde

d. strawberry redhead

e. coppery red-brown

f. red

g. red-black

h. other (please specify) _____

♀ skin color

47. How would you describe your skin color?

a. black (ebony)

d. reddish

b. dark brown

e. olive

c. brown

f. pinkish (rosy)

g. yellowish (peachy)   i. creamy white

h. white   j. other (please specify)

_____

48. If you have freckles, are they

a. red-brown

b. charcoal

c. I have freckles, but I am not sure of their color

♀ wardrobe colors

49. Which of these colors, as a group, have brought you the most compliments throughout your life?

a. black, pure white, clear red, true green

b. gray-blue, plum, powder blue

c. mustard, dark brown, moss green

d. peach, light clear gold, light aqua

50. Which brown do you think looks best on you?

a. golden tan

b. rose brown

c. taupe

d. dark chocolate brown

e. no browns are flattering

f. other (please specify) _____

51. Which green do you wear best?

a. olive

b. true green

c. bright, clear, yellow-green

d. deep blue green

e. no greens are flattering

f. other (please specify) _____

52. *Which colors do you feel you should not wear near your face?*

a. orange

b. black

c. bright golden yellow

d. golden tan

e. navy

f. gold

g. purple

h. burgundy

i. red

j. gray

53. *Do you think you look better in*

a. blue-based colors: cool colors (e.g., burgundy, blue-green)

b. yellow-based colors: warm colors (e.g., peach, camel)

54. *Which of the following do you think looks better on you?*

a. muted or gray colors (e.g., blue denim, dusty rose, smoky green)

b. clear colors (e.g., true blue, bright red, emerald green)

55. *Do you look better in*

a. high contrast color combinations (e.g., black and white, ivory with navy, a light color next to a dark color)

b. low contrast color combinations (e.g., "dyed-to-match" all soft colors, different shades of blue)

For questions 56 to 66, write your answer in the space provided.
56. *What color clothing do you tend to reach for first in your closet?*

_____

57. *If you had to wear the same outfit for several days in a row, what color would you like it to be?*

_____

58. *If you were invited to lunch with an important and powerful person, what color outfit would you wear?*

_____

59. *Think of one outfit that you recently saw in a store or in a magazine and that you thought you would like to have. What color was it?*

_____

60. *Think of several outfits that you have worn that have always brought you compliments. What colors were they?*

_____

61. *Think of someone whose clothing you admire. What colors does he or she usually wear?*

_____

62. *What colors make you feel your best?*

_____

63. *Have you tried on something recently that you liked but were afraid to buy? What color was it?*

_____

64. *What two colors predominate in your wardrobe?*

_____

65. *What colors in addition to those listed in question 64 do you own in any quantity?*

_____

66. *What color do you associate with each of the following adjectives?*

a. sad _____

b. happy _____

What color makes you feel your best?

c. masculine _____

d. feminine _____

e. powerful _____

f. weak _____

g. aggressive _____

h. submissive _____

i. sophisticated _____

j. elementary _____

k. conservative _____

l. progressive _____

m. boring _____

n. exciting _____

o. optimistic _____

p. pessimistic _____

q. individualistic _____

r. ordinary _____

67. *In question 66, circle the letter designating those adjectives that you would like to have applied to you.*

68. *Are you interested in redefining your wardrobe in terms of the colors that work best on you?*

a. yes

b. no

c. maybe eventually

c. undecided

♀ consider the total look

69. *For makeup, do you prefer*

a. a natural look

b. a dramatic look

c. a lot of makeup but subtly applied

d. blue-based colored blush and lipstick (e.g., plum, burgundy, mahogany)

e. yellow-based colored blush and lipstick (e.g., orange, peach, rust)

f. mascara on upper and lower lashes

g. eye shadow to match your outfit

h. eye shadow to match your eye color

i. no eye shadow

j. changing makeup with what is in fashion

k. lining your eyes

l. using lip liner

m. "chapstick" rather than lipstick

n. no makeup

o. experimenting, trying new looks

p. wearing it at night only

q. other (please specify) _____

70. *If you could only take two pieces of makeup with you on a trip, what would they be?*

a. _____

b. _____

71. *Regarding your hair, do you prefer it*

a. long   e. curly

b. short   f. wavy

c. to the chin   g. kinky

d. to the shoulder   h. straight

If you could take only two pieces of makeup with you on a trip, what would they be?

i.   frosted

j.   bleached

k.   dyed

l.   in a classic style

m. in a current, fashionable style

n.   other (please specify)

_____

72. *For the fabrics listed below:*

▶ *Place an "X" to the left of the fabrics that you generally like.*
▶ *Go back and circle the letter designating the fabrics that you are uncomfortable wearing.*
▶ *Go back and place a letter "A" to the right of any to which you are allergic.*

_____ a. cotton

_____ b. silk

_____ c. linen

_____ d. wool

_____ e. synthetics

_____ f. blends

_____ g. metallic

_____ h. fur

_____ i. leather and suede

_____ j. velour

_____ k. challis

_____ l. crepe

_____ m. taffeta

_____ n. satin

_____ o. velvet

_____ p. knits

_____ q. gabardine

_____ r. double knits

_____ s. hopsacking

_____ t. corduroy

_____ u. fleece

_____ v. other (please specify)

_____

73. *For the jewelry listed below:*

▶ *Place an "X" to the left of the jewelry you prefer to wear.*
▶ *Go back and circle the letter designating the kinds of jewelry that you wear when dressed professionally.*

_____ a. costume

_____ b. genuine gold,
          silver, platinum,
          copper, brass

_____ c. unique statements

_____ d. precious and
          semiprecious stones
          (e.g., diamond, ruby,
          carnelian, jade)

_____ e. pearls

_____ f. none

_____ g. other (please specify)

_____

74. *For the shoe styles listed below:*

▶ *Place an "X" in front of the shoe style you prefer for daytime wear.*
▶ *Go back and circle the letter designating each style you cannot or do not like to wear.*

_____ a. what is in style

_____ b. sling back

_____ c. pump, closed
   toe and heel

_____ d. open toe

_____ e. high heel

_____ f. low heel

_____ g. flat

_____ h. pointed toe

_____ i. round toe

_____ j. lace

_____ k. slip on

_____ l. sandal

_____ m. buckle

_____ n. with strap

_____ o. boot

_____ p. other (please specify)

_____

For questions 75 to 78, circle the letter of each response that pertains to you.

75. *For a daytime purse, do you prefer*

a. shoulder bag

b. hand bag

c. envelope

d. briefcase/purse combination

e. no purse

f. other (please specify) _____

76. What type of underpants do you prefer wearing?

a. bikini

b. hip-hugger (three-quarter pants)

c. briefs (to the waist)

d. thong

e. french cut (high leg)

77. Which apply to you?

a. You are particular about your underwear.

b. Your underwear is covered up, so you do not worry about it.

c. When you feel like you need to buy something to cheer you up, you buy underwear.

d. You take great care with your nightgown or pajamas, robe, and slippers.

e. When you are dressed in your power suit and want to feel feminine, you wear lacy lingerie.

f. It would be nice to be able to afford lots of lovely underwear.

g. Underwear is necessary, but you should not spend a lot of money on it.

h. You wear no bra.

i. You wear a "nothing" bra.

j. You wear a padded bra.

k. You wear a support bra.

78. I . . .

a. often wear scarves or ties.

b. like scarves or ties on others, but not on myself.

c. wish I knew more about tying scarves or ties.

d. never wear scarves or ties to work.

e. wear scarves or ties occasionally.

f. wear scarves only when they are in style.

I wish I knew more about tying scarves.

♀ roles in life

79. Describe your favorite outfit for work or an important meeting.

_____

_____

_____

80. Think of someone you admire professionally and describe his or her typical outfit.

_____

_____

_____

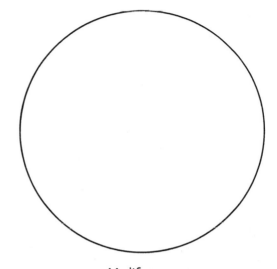

My life now.

81. ▸ *Divide the circle at right into a pie, with each slice representing each of your present roles in life.*
  ▸ *Write each role in the slice of pie.*
  ▸ *Draw a line to each slice and list outside of the circle the types of clothing you need for each role.*

82. Do the same for your life 5 years from now.

♀ get organized

83. Circle the letter of the answer that pertains to you. More than one may apply. When do you shop?

a. at sales

b. whenever I'm blue and need cheering up

c. to reward myself when I reach goals

d. I do it all in two shopping trips a year, usually in fall and spring.

e. When I'm out anyway getting clothes for the children, I shop for myself.

f. when I need something in particular.

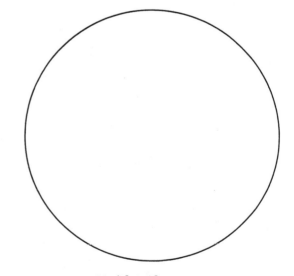

My life in five years.

g. very rarely

h. never

i. other (please specify) _____

84. ▶ *Place an "X" in front of those places you spend most of your time now.*
  ▶ *Go back and circle the letter of the places you anticipate spending most of your time in the future.*

_____ a. office   _____ e. classroom

_____ b. home   _____ f. meetings

_____ c. car   _____ g. other (please specify)

_____ d. studio   _____

85. ▶ *Place an "X" to the left of each description of yourself today.*
  ▶ *Go back and circle the letter of each description of yourself in the future.*

_____ a. executive _____ g. traveler

_____ b. mother   _____ h. student

_____ c. wife   _____ i. secretary

_____ d. fundraiser _____ j. volunteer

_____ e. artist   _____ k. professional

_____ f. theatergoer _____ l. other (please specify)

              _____

86. *When you pack your suitcase, do you take*

a. everything just in case

b. just essentials

c. nonwrinkle clothing

d. clothing that will need ironing

e. something for all weather possibilities

87. When you travel, do you travel

a. for business

b. socially

88. When you carry a purse or briefcase, do you carry

a. Band-Aids, aspirin, Tums, mints, barrettes

b. essentials only

c. I do not carry a purse or briefcase.

89. Which pertain to you?

a. I do not mind ironing.

b. I hate to iron.

c. I will pay to have clothing pressed so I can have natural fibers.

d. I do not mind spending money to have silk blouses cleaned.

e. I prefer easy-care fabrics.

f. I will send a clean item to the cleaners just to get it ironed.

I do not mind ironing.

90. *How much money are you comfortable spending on clothing in a six-month period?*

a. less than $200

b. $200–$500

c. $500–$1,000

d. more than $1,000

91. *If the cost and convenience of purchasing items of clothing were the same, would you prefer*

a. ready-made clothing

b. tailor-made clothing

c. no preference

92. *Where or how do you get most of your clothes?*

a. one store in my home town

b. several stores in my home town

c. in other cities when I travel

d. from catalogues

e. as gifts

f. have them sewn for me

g. sew them myself

h. other (please specify) _____

93. *When you dress for work or an important meeting, which of the following do you feel comfortable wearing?*

a. separates (skirts or slacks and blouses and jackets)

b. dresses alone

c. dresses and jackets

d. two-piece suits

e. three-piece suits

f. sports clothes

g. jumpers

h. pants suits

i. other (please specify) _____

94. ▶ *Place an "X" to the left of each type of clothing you wear around the house (when not dressed professionally).*
    ▶ *Go back and circle the letter of each type of clothing you would prefer wearing around the house (when not dressed professionally).*

_____ a. nice, washable jeans or slacks and sweater/shirt

_____ b. jean or casual skirt and sweater/shirt

_____ c. grubbies

_____ d. house dress

_____ e. knit separates

_____ f. jogging suit or other exercise clothes

_____ g. nonwashable sportswear

_____ h. other (please describe) _____

95. ▶ *Place an "X" to the left of each type clothing you wear to school.*
    ▶ *Go back and circle the letter of the clothing you would prefer wearing to school.*

_____ a. well-worn, faded clothing

_____ b. what is in style at the time

_____ c. whatever is comfortable

_____ d. whatever is flattering

_____ e. grubbies

_____ f. jogging suit or other exercise clothes

_____ g. other (please describe) _____

_____ h. not applicable

96. *When you entertain at home, do you prefer wearing*

a. casual, sporty clothes

b. exciting, dramatic clothes

c. feminine, romantic clothes

d. classic, simple clothes

e. comfortable clothes

f. other (please specify) _____

97. *What kind of parties do you go to most often?*

a. big parties

b. cocktail parties

c. informal get-togethers with friends

d. business parties

e. fundraisers

f. other (please specify) _____

98. ▶ *Place an "X" to the left of the kinds of clothing you wear to the*
    parties you attend.
    ▶ *Go back and circle the letter of each kind of clothing you would*
    prefer wearing to parties.

_____ a. romantic, feminine, ruffly

_____ b. sexy

_____ c. comfortable

_____ d. dramatic, attention-getting

_____ e. conservative, understated

_____ f. elegant

_____ g. classic, to dress up or down with accessories

_____ h. costume

_____ i. other (please describe) _____

99. *If you were to get rid of good clothing that you never wear, would*
you prefer

a. a tax deduction

b. money from consignment (resold clothing)

100. *Do you have a regular program of exercise?*

a. yes   b. no

If the answer is yes, do you

a. jog   c. swim

b. do aerobic dancing   d. ride a bike

e. play tennis   i. walk

f. play racquetball   j. work out at gym

g. play golf   k. other (please specify)

h. do yoga   _____

101. ▶ *Place an "X" next to each place where you store your casual
        clothes and accessories.*
      ▶ *Go back and circle the letters designating the places you store
        your professional clothing and accessories.*

_____ a. one dresser in bedroom

_____ b. two dressers in bedroom

_____ c. one dresser in a room other than bedroom

_____ d. two dressers in a room other than bedroom

_____ e. two dressers, one in bedroom and the other in another

            room

_____ f. more than two dressers

_____ g. closet in bedroom

_____ h. closet out of bedroom

_____ i. drawers in closet

_____ j. coat closet

_____ k. wardrobe

_____ l. next to the washing machine in the basket

_____ m. other (please explain) _____

For questions 102 to 111 write your answer in the space provided.
102. *List the clothing you need for your exercise program.*

_____

_____

103. *Where do you store the clothes you wear for exercising?*

_____

_____

104. When do you feel best dressed?

_____

_____

105. When do you feel bad in your clothes?

_____

_____

106. If your employer imposes restrictions on your dress, describe them.

_____

_____

107. How do persons dress who are in the position in which you see yourself in five years?

_____

_____

108. Describe your favorite outfit in your most time-consuming role.

_____

_____

109. What section(s) of the newspaper do you read?

_____

_____

110. How many times a day do you change clothes?

_____

_____

111. For each of the following, please state your favorite:

a. laundry _____

b. cleaners _____

c. shoe repair store _____

d. shoe dying store _____

e. clothes dying shop _____

f. magazine _____

g. carpenter _____

h. handyperson _____

i. ironing person _____

j. seamstress/tailor _____

k. catalogues _____

l. stores in your area for

    1) scarves _____

    2) shoes _____

    3) purses _____

    4) jewelry _____

    5) glasses _____

    6) makeup _____

    7) hose/socks _____

    8) coats _____

    9) lingerie _____

    10) hats _____

    11) gloves _____

    12) rainwear _____

    13) bargains _____

    14) professional clothes _____

    15) play clothes _____

    16) sport clothes _____

    17) wardrobe organizers _____

    18) other _____

m. stores in other cities

   1) city _____

      store _____

   2) city _____

      store _____

   3) city _____

      store _____

112. In what areas do you feel you need help?

a. organizing clothes and closet

b. finding the colors that look best on you

Getting assistance with

c. hair

d. glasses

e. shopping (for you, with you, for gifts)

f. shoes

g. ties

h. jewelry

i. travel

j. evening wear

k. business wear

l. the total look

m. improving quality rather than quantity of clothes

n. having clothes custom sewn

o. ridding your closet of unused clothes

p. improving your shopping habits

q. putting together a flexible, versatile wardrobe

r. identifying sales in the area

s. buying clothes that will last for years

t. keeping up with the latest fashion trends

u. providing a wardrobe chart or coding system for your closet to
    show what goes together

v. changing your image

w. discovering and dressing in your own style

x. helping you dress for success

y. making the most of your present wardrobe

We hope you enjoyed this questionnaire! Perhaps you have made
some new discoveries and challenged some old assumptions about
yourself. Now let's translate this data into some workable tools. Remember you are a participant in this book! To assist in your self-
evaluation and in learning to *Dress Smart*, you will be asked to complete exercises and record observations in journal pages within this
book. You can return to these entries as you progress to review your
responses and evaluate your growth.

♂ gather data: men

2

1. Baseball
2. Tennis
3. Law
4.
5.

List five activities in which you participate.

Who are you, and what image do you project? What are your body's assets? What colors work for you? What do you wear, and where do you go? To define the direction your wardrobe should take, you need to take time to study *yourself*. Do not spend a lot of time on this questionnaire. Write down the first thing that comes to your mind. And have fun! We will get analytical later.

♂ evolutionize your look

1. Where are you now in your life/career? List five activities in which you presently participate.

a. _____

b. _____

c. _____

d. _____

e. _____

2. Who is the you in your future? Think of options! Remember your choices are wide open! In five or ten years you may be doing something you have not even heard of today. List what you expect your activities will be in five years.

a. _____

b. _____

c. _____

d. _____

e. _____

In ten years

a. _____

b. _____

c. _____

d. _____

e. _____

3. ▶ Place an "X" in front of the wardrobe styles which best describe you now.
   ▶ Go back and circle the letters indicating the styles you want to enhance.

_____ a. sophisticated		_____ k. individualistic
_____ b. sexy		_____ l. casual, sporty
_____ c. virile		_____ m. earthy
_____ d. preppy		_____ n. smart, but not trendy
_____ e. tailored		_____ o. classic, with flair
_____ f. dramatic		_____ p. tweedy
_____ g. understated, quality		_____ q. clothing as art
_____ h. regal		_____ r. international, ethnic
_____ i. authoritative		_____ s. neutral and natural
_____ j. severe		_____ t. clean and simple

_____ u. conservative   _____ x. western

_____ v. elegant   _____ y. unconventional

_____ w. "my only limitation   _____ z. other (please specify)
         is my imagination"
                                _____

4. ▶ *Place an "X" in front of the key words that describe your image.*
   ▶ *Go back and circle the letters indicating the image you want to project in the future.*

_____ a. dramatic   _____ n. traditional

_____ b. flashy   _____ o. comfortable

_____ c. approachable   _____ p. detailed, accessorized,
                                          finished

_____ d. stylish   _____ q. matching, coordinated

_____ e. at ease   _____ r. colorful

_____ f. energetic   _____ s. unusual, unique

_____ g. enthusiastic   _____ t. professional

_____ h. robust   _____ u. inattentive to detail

_____ i. determined   _____ v. couldn't care less
                                          about clothes

_____ j. masculine   _____ w. careless

_____ k. successful   _____ x. carefree

_____ l. versatile   _____ y. other (please specify)

_____ m. tasteful   _____

For questions 5–19, adapted from Charles Hix,[1] check only one letter per question. Move quickly, trusting your instincts.
5. How ambitious are you?

_____ a. You have long-range plans and are impatient to accomplish them.

_____ b. You dream about a glorious future, but have no specific plans.

_____ c. You temper your goals with a strong dose of realism.

_____ d. You go methodically about your business one step at a

time.

_____ e. You are reasonably content to let time and events run

their course.

6. In what type of atmosphere would you be most content to work?

_____ a. A place where your opinions are taken seriously.

_____ b. A place where you feel free to express your opinions

without fear of criticism.

_____ c. A place where advancement is based on talent.

_____ d. A place where advancement is based on hard work.

_____ e. A place where advancement is based on seniority.

_7. If you worked for a tyrannical boss, how would you most likely
react?_

_____ a. By looking for a job with more class and clout.

_____ b. By dreaming of dynamiting the office while your boss

is inside.

_____ c. By having occasional arguments with your boss and

keeping as much distance from him or her as possible.

_____ d. By resenting your boss but trying to earn respect

through hard work.

_____ e. By complaining about him or her to your buddies.

_8. If all of these positions were offered to you and you had the ability
to perform the necessary duties, which one would you be most happy to
accept?_

_____ a. Chairman of the board of an international

conglomerate.

_____ b. Top man at a Hollywood talent agency.

_____ c. Publisher of a newspaper syndicate.

_____ d. Head of a chain of electronics stores.

_____ e. Owner of an enormous cattle ranch.

9. *Among your working associates, which would you prefer?*

_____ a. To be respected.

_____ b. To be considered clever.

_____ c. To be recognized as someone who will stand up for what is right.

_____ d. To be recognized as someone with a future.

_____ e. To be well liked.

10. *Which of these impressions would you prefer to make on strangers or casual acquaintances?*

_____ a. That you know what you want.

_____ b. That you are free spirited and independent.

_____ c. That you know your way around.

_____ d. That your feet are firmly on the ground.

_____ e. That you are a nice guy.

11. *How are you most likely to react if you feel someone has a poor opinion of you?*

_____ a. You would dismiss that person from your thoughts.

_____ b. You would feel resentful toward the individual and wonder how he got a bad impression.

_____ c. You would treat the person cordially but somewhat coolly, unless you genuinely respect that person, in which case you would try to understand what prompted the misinterpretation.

_____ d. You would try to devise a plan to win the person's approval.

_____ e. You would feel hurt but would believe there is no way
to remedy the situation because you have already tried
your best.

12. *How do you feel when you see a stranger acting or dressing so
eccentrically that other people stop and stare?*

_____ a. You feel slightly dismayed that the onlookers have
nothing better to do with their lives, while averting
your eyes from the spectacle.

_____ b. You feel a bit depressed, remembering with a pang
when someone had once made fun of you long ago.

_____ c. You feel surprised that the onlookers are at all
interested in gaping because the world is filled with
stranger people.

_____ d. You dislike the stranger and wish all such people
would disappear.

_____ e. You feel sorry for the person who is the center of
attention and hope the stranger has not noticed the
crowd's disapproval.

13. *How would you feel if you saw a friend making a fool of himself in
a public place?*

_____ a. You would be surprised that the friend lacked the
sense to keep himself under control.

_____ b. You would queasily hope that your friend would not
notice your presence and draw you into the scene.

_____ c. You would feel embarrassed by your friend's foolish
antics, wondering what had precipitated them.

_____ d. You would feel slightly angered at—and disappointed
in—your friend for making a fool of himself.

_____ e. You would feel sorry for your friend and would look for some way to explain his behavior.

14. If you heard someone making a critical remark about your clothes, what would you most likely do?

_____ a. You would first consider the source.

_____ b. You would think that the meddler knows nothing about current fashion and then evaluate yourself against that person's appearance.

_____ c. You would wonder why your critic felt the need to comment on your attire.

_____ d. You would look at your compatriot's clothing to see in what way he was dressing differently.

_____ e. You would wonder why you were singled out for criticism, then decide you are who you are and forget the incident.

15. If an old friend told you that a recently made friend had spread a nasty—and untrue—rumor about you, how would you feel?

_____ a. You would momentarily be angered but then decide you had misjudged the new friend and write that person off.

_____ b. You would feel upset with yourself for being duped by the new friend, but then decide that there are many other entertaining people in the world to spend time with. Still, the wounds would take a while to heal.

_____ c. Your first reaction would be to confront the new friend, but then you would feel puzzled and wonder why the old friend had told you instead of quashing the rumor himself.

_____ d. You would feel annoyed that the person had ever won
       your trust and then wonder how many of your
       acquaintances had heard the gossip and how many of
       them believed it.

_____ e. You would feel betrayed by the new friend and, unable
       to comprehend such hypocrisy, would never forgive
       and forget.

16. *How do you react to pettiness in others?*

_____ a. You are angered by it and are tempted to call their
       attention to the sin of small mindedness.

_____ b. You like to see petty people get their comeuppance
       and sometimes react sarcastically to them.

_____ c. You dislike pettiness but philosophically accept it as
       common human frailty; in practice, however, you avoid
       petty people.

_____ d. Pettiness in others can prompt pettiness in you,
       although you are apt to criticize other people's
       pettiness when with your friends.

_____ e. Pettiness of any kind saddens you, but you search for
       everyone's better side.

17. *Other than family members, who would you most likely ask for
advice when facing a difficult personal decision?*

_____ a. Someone who has special or inside information
       pertaining to the situation.

_____ b. Someone who has been faced with a similar decision.

_____ c. A disinterested party whose intelligence you respect.

_____ d. A number of associates to reach a consensus.

_____ e. Your best friend.

18. *How are you likely to respond when introduced to a stranger?*

_____ a. You will be polite and will set the tone for the conversation, taking the opportunity to size up the newcomer.

_____ b. You will smile generously and converse while trying to figure out whether the new acquaintance seems to like you or not.

_____ c. You will trust your intuition, and if you feel drawn to the individual, you will try extra hard to make friends.

_____ d. You will tend to hold back judgment until learning more about him.

_____ e. If common interests are not established by the setting or the group, you will often have difficulty deciding what to talk about and will allow the other person to take the lead.

19. *Which of the following types of people are you most likely to get along with?*

_____ a. People with very definite opinions, particularly if their opinions are similar to your own.

_____ b. People who like to have a good time and are amusing to be with.

_____ c. People who are well versed on many subjects and are good conversationalists.

_____ d. People who share similar interests to your own.

_____ e. People who are warm and considerate.

20. *Which of the following cars would you be likely to choose?*

_____ a. Cadillac

_____ b. Porsche Convertible

_____ c. Toyota Prius hybrid

_____ d. Buick Sedan

_____ e. Jeep

21. Rank the statements below by putting a numeral one (1) on the line beside the statement with which you most strongly agree. Continue to rank the statements 2–3–4–5–6–7, so that seven is beside the statement with which you most strongly disagree. This may be challenging, but it will force you to prioritize. Bear with us!

_____ a. The first thing I look at in regard to clothing is price.

_____ b. I like to know about the various fibers and textures and designs of fabrics.

_____ c. Clothes have to be comfortable for me to wear them.

_____ d. A beautiful color frequently influences my buying decision.

_____ e. I think men should dress to enhance their masculinity, and women should dress to enhance their femininity.

_____ f. I try to dress similarly to others in the group I am in.

_____ g. I notice if someone is better dressed than I am.

22. Rank the statements below in the same manner as in question 21: one (1), beside the item with which you most strongly agree, through seven (7), beside the statement with which you most strongly disagree. Again, do your best to choose.

_____ a. I usually buy a few things that can be worn interchangeably.

_____ b. The symbolism of garments contributes to appearance and sends messages to the observer.

_____ c. I will not wear clothes that feel too tight, even if they look good that way.

_____ d. I like accessories that are a little different, but beautifully designed.

I usually buy things that can be worn interchangeably.

_____ e. I am very aware of how my body looks in clothes.

_____ f. I like to be in style, but not to an extreme.

_____ g. I am influenced by labels when I shop.

23. Rank these statements in the same manner as the statements in 21 and 22.

_____ a. When I buy clothing, I always consider the care it will require.

_____ b. The history of costume fascinates me.

_____ c. I am miserable if my clothes are not warm enough or cool enough.

_____ d. A well-cut and well-designed garment is important to me.

_____ e. Poor posture can ruin the appearance of nice clothes.

_____ f. I think dress codes for professional situations are a good idea.

_____ g. I like to be the first to wear a new style.

♂ enrich your raw materials

There are ways to dress to accentuate the positive and play down the negative features of your body. The following questions are designed to help you analyze your raw materials.

24. Circle the letter before each of the following that applies to you.

a. round face

b. square jaw

c. long, thin face

d. sway back

e. heavy thighs

f. weight changes a lot

g. one hip higher than the other

h. one shoulder higher than the other

i. high waist

j. long waist

k. unsure

l. none of the above

m. other (please specify)

_____

▶ *In questions 25–44, place an "X" to the left of the body characteristics that best describe you.*

▶ *Go back and circle the letter that indicates what you consider ideal.*

25. Body Size

_____ a. slender

_____ b. average

_____ c. plump

_____ d. big

26. Height

_____ a. short

_____ b. average

_____ c. tall

27. Foot Shape

_____ a. narrow

_____ b. average

_____ c. wide

28. Leg Shape

_____ a. slender

_____ b. average

_____ c. full

29. Leg Length

_____ a. short

_____ b. medium

_____ c. long

30. Derrière Shape

_____ a. flat

_____ b. rounded

_____ c. protruding

31. Hip Size

_____ a. narrow

_____ b. medium

_____ c. wide

32. Stomach

_____ a. flat

_____ b. rounded

_____ c. protruding

33. Waist Size

_____ a. small

_____ b. medium

_____ c. large

34. Hand Size

_____ a. small

_____ b. medium

_____ c. large

35. Arm Length

_____ a. short

_____ b. medium

_____ c. long

36. Arm Size

_____ a. thin

_____ b. average

_____ c. full

37. Chest Size

_____ a. small

_____ b. medium

_____ c. large

_____ d. extra large

38. Shoulders

_____ a. narrow

_____ b. average

_____ c. broad

_____ d. rounded or sloping

_____ e. broad or square

39. Neck

_____ a. short

_____ b. average

_____ c. long

_____ d. narrow

_____ e. broad

40. Teeth

_____ a. dull, yellowish

_____ b. white

_____ c. shiny, pearly

41. Lips

_____ a. thin

_____ b. medium

_____ c. thick

42. Nose Shape

_____ a. flat

_____ b. turned up

_____ c. hooked

_____ d. narrow

_____ e. wide

_____ f. straight

_____ g. long

43. Eye Size

_____ a. small

_____ b. medium

_____ c. large

44. Hair Type

_____ a. straight

_____ b. wavy

_____ c. curly

_____ d. kinky

45. *Do you want to look*

a. older

b. younger

c. taller

d. thinner

e. shorter

f. heavier

g. yourself

h. other (please specify)

_____

46. *List your body assets.*

_____

_____

47. *List your body challenges.*

_____

_____

Do you want to look . . .

♂ employ color

The correct colors are extremely important to any wardrobe. Each individual has certain colors that work best on him. The following questions are designed to help determine how you can use color to your best advantage. In response to questions 48–63, circle the letters for the answer that pertains to you.

♂ eye color

48. *What is the color of your eyes? In bright daylight, study your eyes in a mirror and describe the colors and patterns you observe. (You might want help from a friend on this one.)*

_____

_____

_____

♂ hair color

49. What is the natural color of your hair?

a. blonde

b. brown

c. red

d. gray

e. black

f. other (please specify)

_____

50. If you are a natural blonde, is your natural hair color

a. ash-blonde

b. "mousey" blonde

c. golden blonde

d. platinum blonde

e. flaxen blonde

f. strawberry blonde

g. dark blonde

h. other (please specify)

_____

51. If you have naturally brown hair, is it

a. golden

b. chestnut

c. red-brown

d. "mousey"

e. ash

f. medium

g. dark brown

h. taupe

i. other (please specify)

_____

52. If your hair is naturally gray, would you describe it as

a. silver gray

b. salt and pepper

c. blue gray

d. golden gray

e. premature

f. other (please specify)

_____

53. If your hair is naturally black, would you describe it as

a. red black

b. blue black

c. brown black

d. ebony

e. salt and pepper

f. other (please specify) _____

54. *If you have red in your hair, which of the following best describes it?*

a. red highlights in medium brown hair

b. auburn

c. strawberry blonde

d. strawberry redhead

e. coppery red-brown

f. red

g. red-black

h. other (please specify) _____

♂ skin color

55. *How would you describe your skin color?*

a. black (ebony)

b. dark brown

c. brown

d. reddish

e. pinkish (rosy)

f. yellowish (peachy)

g. white

h. creamy white

i. other (please specify)

_____

56. *If you have freckles, are they*

a. red-brown

b. charcoal

c. I have freckles, but I am not sure of their color

♂ wardrobe colors

57. Which of these colors, as a group, have brought you the most compliments throughout your life?

a. black, pure white, clear red, true green

b. gray-blue, plum, powder blue

c. mustard, dark brown, moss green

d. peach, light clear gold, light aqua

58. Which brown do you think looks best on you?

a. golden tan

b. rose brown

c. dark chocolate brown

d. no browns are flattering

e. other (please specify) _____

59. Which green do you wear best?

a. olive

b. true green

c. bright, clear, yellow-green

d. deep blue green

e. no greens are flattering

f. other (please specify) _____

60. Which colors do you feel you should not wear near your face?

a. orange

b. black

c. bright golden yellow

d. golden tan

e. navy

f. gold

g. purple

h. burgundy

i. red

j. gray

61. *Do you think you look better in*

a. blue-based colors: cool colors (e.g., burgundy, forest green, pure white)

b. yellow-based colors: warm colors (e.g., camel, rust, cream)

62. *Which of the following do you think looks better on you?*

a. muted or gray colors (e.g., blue denim, dusty rose, smoky green)

b. clear colors (e.g., true blue, bright red, emerald green)

63. *Do you look better in*

a. high contrast color combinations (e.g., black with white, ivory with navy, a light color next to a dark color)

b. low contrast color combinations (e.g., "dyed-to-match" all soft colors, different shades of blue)

For questions 64 to 74, write your answer in the space provided.

64. *What color clothing do you tend to reach for first in your closet?*

_____

65. *If you had to wear the same outfit for several days in a row, what color would you like it to be?*

_____

66. *If you were invited to lunch with an important and powerful person, what color clothing would you wear?*

_____

67. *Think of one ensemble that you recently saw in a store or in a magazine and that you thought you would like to have. What color was it?*

_____

68. *Think of colors of clothing that you have worn that have brought you compliments. What colors were they?*

_____

69. *Think of someone whose clothing you admire. What colors does he or she usually wear?*

_____

70. *What colors make you feel your best?*

_____

71. *Have you tried on something recently that you were afraid to buy? What color was it?*

_____

72. *What two colors predominate in your wardrobe?*

_____

73. *What colors in addition to those listed in question 72 do you own in any quantity?*

_____

74. *What color do you associate with each or the following adjectives?*

a. sad _____

b. happy _____

c. masculine _____

d. feminine _____

e. powerful _____

f. weak _____

g. aggressive _____

h. submissive _____

i. sophisticated _____

j. elementary _____

k. conservative _____

l. progressive _____

m. boring _____

n. exciting _____

o. optimistic _____

p. pessimistic _____

q. individualistic _____

r. ordinary _____

♂ consider the total look

75. For the fabrics listed below, please do the following:

▶ *Place an "X" to the left of the fabrics that you like.*
▶ *Go back and circle the letter designating the fabrics that you are uncomfortable wearing.*
▶ *Then, go back and place a letter "A" to the right of any to which you are allergic.*

_____ a. cotton			_____ l. leather and suede
_____ b. silk			_____ m. fur
_____ c. linen			_____ n. metallic
_____ d. wool			_____ o. corduroy
_____ e. synthetics			_____ p. velour
_____ f. blends			_____ q. knits
_____ g. crepe			_____ r. gabardine
_____ h. taffetta			_____ s. double knits
_____ i. satin			_____ t. hopsacking
_____ j. velvet			_____ u. fleece
_____ k. velveteen			_____ v. other (please specify)

_____

76. *For the jewelry listed below:*

▸ *Place an "X" to the left of the jewelry you prefer to wear.*
▸ *Go back and circle the letter designating the kinds of jewelry that you wear when dressed professionally.*

_____ a. ring(s) and   _____ f. chains

     watch only

_____ b. genuine gold,   _____ g. lapel pins

     silver, platinum,

     copper, brass

_____ c. unique statements   _____ h. bracelet

_____ d. precious and   _____ i. pocket watch

     semiprecious stones

     (e.g., diamond, ruby,

     carnelian, jade)

_____ e. tie tack   _____ j. other (please specify)

         _____

77. *For the shoe styles listed below:*

▸ *Place an "X" in front of the shoe style you prefer for daytime wear.*
▸ *Go back and circle the letter designating each style you cannot or do not like to wear.*

_____ a. slip-ons only

_____ b. lace-ups only

_____ c. sporty, cap-toe shoe

_____ d. seamless tie shoe

_____ e. basic oxford lace-up

_____ f. square-toes

_____ g. light colored (taupe, tan, camel, white)

_____ h. multicolored

_____ i. brogues (solid walking shoes with brass eyelets)

_____ j. tassel loafers

_____ k. penny loafers

_____ l. saddle shoes

_____ m. jogging or tennis shoes

_____ n. not-too-heavy wing tips

_____ o. heavy wing tips

_____ p. sandals

_____ q. boots

_____ r. other (please specify) _____

For questions 78 to 81, circle the letter of each response that pertains to you.

78. Do you carry a(n)

a. bag or purse

b. envelope briefcase

c. briefcase with handle

d. no briefcase

e. other (please specify) _____

79. What type of underclothes do you prefer wearing?

a. bikini pants

b. hip-hugger (three-quarter pants)

c. briefs (to the waist)

d. boxer shorts

e. all cotton

f. V-necked undershirts

g. round-necked undershirts

h. tank-top undershirts

i. no undershirts

j. other (please specify) _____

80. Which apply to you?

a. You are particular about your underwear.

b. Your underwear is covered up, so you do not worry about it.

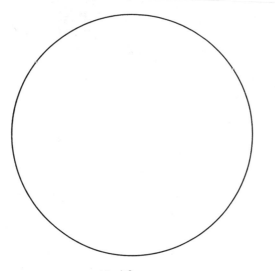

My life now.

c. When you feel like you need to buy something to cheer you up, you buy underwear.

d. You take great care with your pajamas, robe, and slippers.

81. I

a. often wear ties.

b. always wear ties to work.

c. never wear ties to work.

d. like ties on others, but not on myself.

e. wish I knew more about tying ties.

f. wear bowties.

g. wear ascots.

h. wear a certain pattern tie only (please specify) _____.

i. use a certain knot only (please specify) _____.

82. *Describe your favorite clothing for work or an important meeting.*

_____

_____

83. *Think of someone you admire professionally and describe his or her typical clothing.*

_____

_____

84. ▶ *Divide the first circle into a pie, with each slice representing each of your present roles in life.*
 ▶ *Write each role in the slice of pie.*
 ▶ *Draw a line to each slice and list outside of the circle the types of clothing you need for each role.*

85. *Do the same for your life five years from now.*

♂ get organized

86. *Circle the letter of the answer that pertains to you. More than one may apply. When do you shop?*

a. at sales

b. whenever I'm blue and need cheering up

My life in five years.

c. to reward myself when I reach goals

d. I do it all in two shopping trips a year, usually in fall and spring.

e. When I'm out anyway getting clothes for the children, I shop for myself.

f. When I'm shopping with my wife or friend, I shop for myself.

g. when I need something in particular

h. very rarely

i. never

j. other (please specify) _____

87. ▶ Place an "X" in front of those places you spend most of your time now.
   ▶ Go back and circle the letter of the places you anticipate spending most of your time in the future.

_____ a. office   _____ e. classroom

_____ b. home   _____ f. meetings

_____ c. car   _____ g. other (please specify)

_____ d. studio   _____

88. ▶ Place an "X" to the left of each description of yourself today.
   ▶ Go back and circle the letter of each description of yourself in the future.

_____ a. executive   _____ g. traveler

_____ b. father   _____ h. student

_____ c. husband   _____ i. secretary

_____ d. fundraiser   _____ j. volunteer

_____ e. artist   _____ k. professional (please specify) _____

_____ f. theatergoer   _____ l. other (please specify)

                                        _____

89. When you pack your suitcase, do you take

a. everything just in case

b. just essentials

c. nonwrinkle clothing

d. clothing that will need ironing

e. something for all weather possibilities

90. When you travel, do you travel

a. for business

b. socially

91. Which pertains to you?

a. I do not mind ironing.

b. I hate to iron.

c. I will pay to have clothing pressed so I can have natural fibers.

d. I prefer easy-care fabrics and *don't* iron them.

e. I prefer easy-care fabrics and *do* iron them.

f. My mother or girlfriend/significant other irons.

92. How much money are you comfortable spending on clothing in a six-month period?

a. less than $200

b. $200–$500

c. $500–$1,000

d. more than $1,000

93. If the cost and convenience of purchasing items of clothing were the same, would you prefer

a. ready-made clothing

b. tailor-made clothing

c. no preference

94. Where or how do you get most of your clothes?

a. one store in my home town

b. several stores in my home town

c. in other cities when I travel

d. from catalogues

e. as gifts

f. have them hand-tailored

g. other (please specify) _____

95. *When you dress for work or an important meeting, which of the following do you feel comfortable wearing?*

a. separates (slacks and shirts and jackets)

b. two-piece suits

c. three-piece suits

d. sports clothes

e. other (please specify) _____

96. ▶ *Place an "X" to the left of each type of clothing you wear around the house (when not dressed professionally).*
  ▶ *Go back and circle the letter of each type of clothing you would prefer wearing around the house (when not dressed professionally).*

_____ a. nice, washable jeans or slacks and sweater/shirt

_____ b. grubbies

_____ c. jogging suit or other exercise clothes

_____ d. nonwashable sportswear

_____ e. other (please describe) _____

97. ▶ *Place an "X" to the left of each type clothing you wear to school.*
  ▶ *Go back and circle the letter of the clothing you would prefer wearing to school.*

_____ a. well-worn, faded clothing

_____ b. what is in style at the time

_____ c. whatever is comfortable

_____ d. whatever is flattering

_____ e. grubbies

_____ f. jogging suit or other exercise clothes

_____ g. other (please describe) _____

_____ h. not applicable

98. When you entertain at home, do you prefer wearing

a. casual, sporty clothes

b. exciting, dramatic clothes

c. masculine clothes

d. comfortable clothes

e. other (please describe) _____

99. What kind of parties do you go to most often?

a. big parties

b. cocktail parties

c. informal get-togethers with friends

d. business parties

e. fundraisers

f. other (please specify) _____

100. ▸ *Place an "X" to the left of each kind of clothing you wear to parties.*
    ▸ *Go back and circle the letter of each kind of clothing you would prefer wearing to parties.*

_____ a. sexy

_____ b. comfortable

_____ c. dramatic, attention-getting

_____ d. conservative, understated

_____ e. elegant

_____ f. classic, to dress up or down with accessories

_____ g. other (please describe) _____

101. *If you were to get rid of good clothing that you never wear, would you prefer*

a. a tax deduction

b. money from consignment (resold clothing)

102. *Do you have a regular program of exercise?*

a. yes   b. no

If the answer is yes, do you

a. jog   g. play racquetball

b. do aerobic dancing   h. play golf

c. swim   i. do yoga

d. ride a bike   j. work out at the gym

e. play tennis   k. other (please specify)

f. walk   _____

103. ▸ *Place an "X" next to each place where you store your casual*
         clothes and accessories.
      ▸ *Go back and circle the letters designating the places you store*
         your professional clothing and accessories.

_____ a. one dresser in bedroom

_____ b. two dressers in bedroom

_____ c. one dresser in a room other than bedroom

_____ d. two dressers in a room other than bedroom

_____ e. two dressers, one in bedroom and the other in another

            room

_____ f. more than two dressers

_____ g. closet in bedroom

_____ h. closet out of bedroom

_____ i. drawers in closet

_____ j. coat closet

_____ k. wardrobe

_____ l. other (please explain) _____

For questions 104 to 113, write your answer in the space provided:

104. List the clothing you need for your exercise program:

_____

_____

105. Where do you store the clothes you wear for exercising?

_____

106. When do you feel best dressed?

_____

107. When do you feel bad in your clothes?

_____

108. If your employer imposes restrictions on your dress, describe them.

_____

_____

109. How do persons dress who are in the position in which you see yourself in five years?

_____

110. Describe your favorite outfit in your most time-consuming role.

_____

111. What section(s) of the newspaper do you read?

_____

112. How many times a day do you change clothes?

_____

What sections of the newspaper do you read?

113. *For each of the following, please state your favorite:*

a. laundry _____

b. cleaners _____

c. shoe repair store _____

d. clothes dying shop _____

e. magazine _____

f. catalogue _____

g. carpenter _____

h. handyperson _____

i. ironing person _____

j. seamstress/tailor _____

k. stores in your area for

    1) ties _____

    2) shoes _____

    3) jewelry _____

    4) glasses _____

    5) toiletries _____

    6) socks _____

    7) coats _____

    8) hats _____

    9) gloves _____

    10) rainwear _____

    11) bargains _____

    12) professional clothes _____

    13) play clothes _____

    14) sport clothes _____

    15) wardrobe organizers _____

    16) other _____

l. stores in other cities

    1) city _____

       store _____ _____

    2) city _____

       store _____

    3) city _____

       store _____

114. In what areas do you feel you need help?

a. organizing clothes and closet

b. finding the colors that look best on you

Getting assistance with

c. hair

d. glasses

e. shopping (for you, with you, for gifts)

f. shoes

g. ties

h. jewelry

i. travel

j. evening wear

k. business wear

l. the total look

m. improving quality rather than quantity of clothes

n. having clothes custom sewn

o. ridding your closet of unused clothes

p. improving your shopping habits

q. putting together a flexible, versatile wardrobe

r. identifying sales in the area

s. buying clothes that will last for years

t. keeping up with the latest fashion trends

u. providing a wardrobe chart or coding system for your closet to

    show what goes together

v. changing your image

w. discovering and dressing in your own style

x. helping you dress for success

y. making the most of your present wardrobe

We hope you enjoyed this questionnaire! Perhaps you have made
some new discoveries and challenged some old assumptions about
yourself. Now let's translate this data into some workable tools. Remember you are a participant in this book! To assist in your self-
evaluation and in learning to *Dress Smart*, you will be asked to complete exercises and record observations in the journal pages within
this book. You can return to these entries as you progress to review
your responses and evaluate your growth.

endnote

1. Reprinted from *How to Dress Your Man* by Charles Hix, © 1981 by
    Charles Hix, Crown Publishers, Inc.

market yourself

3

George wanted more than anything to be president of the Student Senate but even though he had voted once, and had been elected secretary of his fraternity, he feared that the two candidates running against him had the edge. Both had looks and brains, and one even had been captain of the volleyball team. She had executive experience!

One afternoon, while shopping for pretzels at the Mini-Mart, George spotted a display, "The Flag! Wear this pin with pride and always be a winner!" In small print the display card explained that The Flag's power would make its owner seem smart, talented, and irresistible, while adversaries would tremble and self-destruct. The secret lay in wearing the pin close to one's heart and quietly letting its secret work. George bought it (and purchased the pin too!). He pinned The Flag squarely on his left lapel and felt smarter and more talented already!

The candidates' debate ensued. The hall was hushed and George sat confidently at the table and said nothing while his agitated opponents argued, ranted, babbled, and basically said nothing as well. The debate ended. Flashbulbs went off. People applauded. George just knew he had won. Some spectators thought George had won too, and several even said they would vote for him! The pin was working!

The election came, and it was close enough to be confusing; but George, knowing his "Flag" was firmly in place, finally spoke up and said, "Hey . . . this is silly! Everybody knows I'm supposed to be the winner!" His confidence was at an all-time high. He looked like a leader and he felt like a leader. He had the pin that would make him win. After several recounts, the election judges agreed. George was proclaimed President!

That night, when George looked in the mirror to congratulate himself, he noticed that The Flag pin was missing. It had fallen off his jacket and he hadn't even known it. When the campus paper published the picture of George taken at the debate, it looked as if his pin had disappeared already. How could that be?

It wasn't The Flag pin that had made George the winner. It was his belief in himself—the way he held his head and the way he looked as if he deserved to win—that got him what he wanted. There is a lot of power in perception!

It wasn't The Flag pin at all that had gotten George elected.

the power of perception

Looking successful is often the first step to being successful. Psychological studies show that the way we perceive ourselves has a lot to do with how others perceive us. If people think they are worth knowing, they will be. If they think they look good, they will.

If we don't already have a positive self-concept, how do we get one? Jefferson Airplane sang "You're only pretty as you feel. You're only pretty as you feel inside."

To feel good about ourselves, do we see a psychologist or psychiatrist and get the *internals* fixed up? Do we spend weeks or months or years on our feelings and then the external will be as we like it? That certainly is one way. Another way to begin is to work on the *external*. And the results are immediate. What you do to the external becomes internalized. If you look good, you feel good. If you feel good, you act more confidently and your performance improves. You get that promotion or that job or that position you have been wanting. Yes, there is a lot of power in perception. Perception is your image. And perception is what is. True or not, what people see is what they believe.

Your image is a combination of your appearance and behavior. It includes your attitudes and how you approach the world, the work you do, and the pride you take in it. Everywhere you go, your image speaks loudly and clearly, for your image *is* you in the eyes and minds of others.

COMPONENTS OF YOUR IMAGE:

1. Self-concept
2. Standards of excellence
3. Personal attitudes
4. Etiquette
5. Verbal communication skills
   a. Grammar
   b. Sentence structure
   c. Vocabulary
   d. Precision
6. Body language
   a. Facial expression
   b. Eye contact
   c. Gestures
   d. Posture
7. Paralanguage (How you sound)
   a. Rate
   b. Pitch
   c. Volume
   d. Animation
   e. Vocalized pauses
   f. Quality
   g. Articulation
8. Appearance
   a. Gender
   b. Age
   c. Hair and skin color
   d. Body type
   e. Grooming
   f. Clothes
   g. Artifacts (props)

It is important to be aware of the image you project, for only then can you work on your weaknesses and create the image you desire.

Dress Smart is about one aspect of image: appearance. You may want to check the bibliography for sources on the other seven image components.

Dr. Albert Mehrabian and other communication experts have concluded that effective communication has three basic components: appearance and body language (the way we look), paralanguage (the way we sound), and words (what we say.) Which of these three do you think is most significant? The experts break it down as follows:

> 55% the way we look
> 38% the way we sound
> 7% the words we use
> _____
> 100% effective communication

It is not that our words are unimportant! It's just that people may not stick around long enough to hear our words if they have already decided by the way we look and sound that we are not someone who is credible.

Companies and individuals spend billions of dollars a year to present their products. Of that amount, millions are spent on packaging that sells. The outside of something must make us want to know more about the inside. *Dress Smart* is about personal packaging. Good things come in good packages.

Modern life is fast. Our contacts are brief. We are constantly making snap visual assessments. Even at the supermarket we unconsciously categorize people: What kind of car they drive, how much education they have, to what social strata they belong. We may even make some assumptions about a woman's morality if she is wearing a clinging low-cut halter top or a man's if he is wearing tight leather pants and gold chains. We never know when we might meet our future boss, or the person who will give us a needed loan. We must market ourselves at all times!

Research results vary on the exact time, but a first impression is made somewhere between a half a minute and four minutes after the first contact. If that first impression is good, it is like putting money into a skyrocketing stock. It will pay great dividends. If that impression is bad, it will be an uphill battle to dispel. And, people tend to skew all subsequent data to fit that first impression.

Have you ever met someone you thought you did not want to get to know better? Then you were forced to be with that person—say on a committee or at the office—and you found that person to be wonderful. You enjoyed being with that person so much that after 10 or 20 meetings you wondered why you ever had the negative feelings in the first place?

This seems to happen frequently. As unfair as it is, people are sizing us up all the time and deciding whether or not we are worth their while. We want to be certain to send a positive and appropriate first impression.

evaluate your self-image

You can gain insights about yourself by keeping a daily journal of your activities, clothing decisions, and the responses of others to your appearance. Let's begin this process by taking a few minutes to answer the five questions in "Appropriate Dress" and completing the chart "Experiment with Your Packaging." Then, answer the "Experiment" questions at the end of every day to see if a pattern emerges.

Sometimes it helps to observe others with whom you come in contact, but do not know very well. As best you can, complete the chart "Observing Others." Is there any way you can check the accuracy of your information?

Even at the supermarket, we unconsciously categorize people.

● ●

Appropriate dress

1. Tomorrow, who will see me?

_____

_____

_____

_____

_____

_____

_____

_____

2. What will they see?

_____

_____

_____

_____

_____

3. There is no such thing as neutral clothing. Your clothing speaks. In fact, it may even shout. Is your clothing saying what you intend it to say?

_____

_____

_____

_____

_____

4. What are you wearing right this minute?

_____

_____

_____

_____

_____

5. Why did you choose these clothes?

_____

_____

_____

_____

_____

_____

● ●

Experiment with your packaging

Complete the two left columns now. Then, at a set time at the end of each day, write yes or no in the remaining six columns.

What did you wear today?		Have you been treated as a person of authority and credibility?				Have your authority and credibility been challenged?	
Day	Clothing	Superior/ Teachers	Coworkers/ Students	Subordinates	Service Persons	By Men	By Women

● ●

Observing others

What can you tell about strangers? Can you check your accuracy?

			If employed	
Name	Age	Profession	Company	Annual salary

professional dress

Professional image skills are not instinctive. They can be learned. You are now on your way to learning what works.

"Professional" is defined by *Webster's Dictionary* as, "of or pertaining to a profession: one of a number of occupations or vocations involving special learning and carrying a certain social prestige; the occupation to which one devotes oneself; a calling; as contrasted to an amateur; following a line of conduct as though it were a profession."

You can be a professional student, a professional volunteer, a professional parent, a professional artist, a professional businessperson. And you obviously won't dress the same way for each of those roles.

A lot has been written on dress, most of it by successful, well-dressed persons with excellent taste. But little has been written on *professional* dress, and very little is based on research.

Historically, men have had solid role models for dress and behavior in a business environment. If you are a businesswoman, however, you may have had few role models and may be confused as to what works on your job. What increases your credibility and authority? How can you dress to appear friendly and approachable?

John T. Molloy wrote the first authoritative book, *Dress for Success,* in 1975. He realized the need for this book when he went to a restaurant one day to meet with three businesswomen, and he could not visually identify who these women were. His subsequent studies showed the need for a woman's "uniform." A woman needs to be identified as a businesswoman, if that is what she is. For some people a uniform is simple, requiring little thought. For right-brained creative persons, wearing uniforms is enough to make the skin crawl.

But Molloy's research is sound. It has been carefully scrutinized by the corporations that funded it. We at least need to know the rules before we break them. Perhaps we need to change our terminology from "uniform" to "career apparel."

dressing successfully

We need to consider what we will be doing a day in advance and plan accordingly. The matched suit will not always be necessary. In fact, sometimes it is ill-advised, that is, not good for sociability at parties or church or in a casual business environment. But a jacket, especially a traditional blazer, will always help us project power. The jacket has been the cloak of authority since ancient kings and rulers wore caps and jackets to set themselves apart from their subjects. Today, if you put your sportcoat on with your jeans, you will increase your authority. Just think of those days when you could use that extra power at softball practice or a scout meeting.

Your career apparel depends on your "profession." Persons in advertising would not wear dark gray suits, white shirts, and black shoes. They need to show more creativity by adding a wonderful pocket square, scarf, tie, or belt and perhaps changing the jacket to a textured sportcoat or cardigan. Similarly, professional volunteers should not effectively wear high-authority career apparel to work in an elementary school (unless they are feeling completely out of control).

See if you can complete the chart, "How Do You Want to Be Perceived Today." The answers follow. How did you do? Then, for each day's activities, ask yourself, "Who will see me?" "What will they see?" Use the information in the charts to help you create the image you want to project for each day's activities. Keep a journal of

A banker dresses differently from a person in advertising.

● ●

How do you want to be perceived today?

Authoritative Austere Standoffish Formal	Influential Friendly Approachable Casual
Dark suit	L_ _ _ _ Suit
Matching s _ _ _	Sport jacket and skirt/slacks
Jacket Buttoned	Jacket u _ _ _ _ _ _ _ _
Jacket o _	Jacket off
Tie o _	Tie off
Tie tied tightly at neck	Tie tied slightly _ w _ _ _ _ _ m neck
Light shirt (white, pale blue) with d_ _ _ suit	Pale yellow shirt with n_ _ _ jacket, blue shirt with k_ _ _ _ / c _ _ _ _ / t _ _ jacket
Shirt buttoned to top	Shirt un _ _ _ _ _ _ _ top b_ _ _ _ _
Hair exact, shoes precise _ _ shi_ _ _	Hair casual, inf _ _ _ _ _ shoes
Hard, crisp fabrics: gaba _ _ _ _ _ s, tw _ _ _ s	Soft t_ _ _ _ _ _ _: tweeds, c _ _ _ _ _ _ _ , k _ _ ts
Solids	Prints, p l _ _ _ _
Maximize height	M _ _ _ _ _ _ height

your clothing choices, purposes, and results. Refer back to the chart "Experimenting with Your Packaging" on page 71. Did your in-creased awareness affect how you were treated by others? Record your responses and then check your answers.

● ●

How do you want to be perceived today?

Authoritative Austere Standoffish Formal	Influential Friendly Approachable Casual
Dark suit	Light suit
Matching suit	Sport jacket and skirt/slacks
Jacket buttoned	Jacket unbuttoned
Jacket on	Jacket off
Tie on	Tie off
Tie tied tightly at neck	Tie tied slightly away from neck
Light shirt (white, pale blue) with dark suit	Pale yellow shirt with navy jacket, blue shirt with khaki/camel/tan jacket
Shirt buttoned to top	Shirt unbuttoned top button (exposed neck)
Hair exact, shoes precisely shined	Hair casually kept, informal shoes
Hard, crisp fabrics: gabardines, twills	Soft textures: tweeds, corduroys, knits
Solids	Prints, plaids
Maximize height	Minimize height

● ●

Clothing choices, purposes, and results

What I Wore	Why	Result

dress tastefully and flexibly

The most recent literature tends to minimize the suit and encourages adding personal touches. This is exciting and good, as long as what you do to the outfit does not detract from you. Business clothing needs to state "I am here for business," whatever that business might be. Ask yourself each evening when you set out your clothing, "Does this look like I will be dressed for the day at hand? Will it announce that I am dependable, consistent, and reliable?"

The problem with fashion is it changes. People who keep up with the latest fashions will subconsciously be perceived as being changeable themselves. Maybe next week they'll leave for another job, city, or even partner. The classic look is most appropriate for professional women and men. An absence of extremes, simplicity, good taste, and quality are associated with classics. Classic clothing is recommended for most businesses because it allows persons to notice the individual's mind and not the clothing. An image of understated elegance and taste, rather than of wild patterns and vivid colors, keeps an individual focused on the total you, as opposed to a specific feature.

Perhaps you think of yourself as other than a classic type. You can bring a touch of tweedyness or a bit of romance to your understated elegance.

Men have been at this game longer than women. Still, both need to dress credibly for the job at hand. We need to dress so people will notice us, not our clothes; notice our minds, not our bodies. Anything that accentuates sexuality does not work well in any professional situation (except for the "oldest profession"). In fact, anything that calls attention to our femininity or masculinity has been shown to work against us.

We like people who are similar to ourselves. We will be hired or promoted or appointed if we look like we belong. Dress to be included, not excluded. Dress for the job you *want*, not the job you *have*. It makes pragmatic sense to temper the dramatic, if that is your true self, at least while you are at work. You can still add your special touches, but don't let them detract from your wise words. At night time or weekends, let it all hang out, unless you're at the office party!

What if you have a business party after work? Do you wear the career apparel during the day and then go home and change into the social apparel for the evening's event? If you think about your clothing a day ahead, you can plan an outfit that can be changed for the party. Women: remove the jacket and expose the silk blouse,

Who is the more powerful, authoritative, and formal? Who is the more friendly, approachable, and casual?

What should you wear to the weekend company picnic to show you are comfortable, casual, and still professional?

change the belt, jewelry, hose, bag, hairdo, and go to the party then and not later; Men: bring a sweater or a knit shirt or go as you are. The key is to think ahead. It depends on what the party is and what your career apparel is.

What you would wear when you are relaxing with your friends or going to dinner with your beloved would probably be different from what you would wear to a business function. You might not need to market yourself at all to your good friends and you might be presenting yourself as anything *but* businesslike to your intended partner.

If the weekend holds the company picnic, what can you wear to show you are comfortable, casual, and still professional? The best choices are precise, exact clothes: those that look ironed on you, custom made for you. As Dr. Julie White says, "Think Military."

Have you ever been to a casual office party or picnic where you were meeting many people for the first time? Did you observe what people were wearing, their body language, grooming, and props? Does your reaction to those same people today in a business meeting still contain elements of those first impressions? How long does a bad impression last?

dress codes

Lately, we have received invitations with confusing dress code messages. What do the invitations mean? Sometimes your guess is as good as ours, but let's try to decode them.

First, how formal does the invitation look? Consider next who sent the invitation. You might call your host or hostess and find out what he or she is going to wear and take your lead from that. Or think in terms of flexibility: adding or deleting an accessory or a jacket if necessary. On the facing page are some standard interpretations or dress codes.

business casual

The term "business casual" is frequently bantered about. We used to just have "casual Friday." Now, more often, we might have a dress-up meeting, but the rest of our lives is business casual. Business casual does not mean tattered blue jeans, sneakers, sweatshirts, muscles shirts, or halter tops, but can vary in interpretations from

DRESS CODES

Black tie formal:
    tuxedo for men
    long dress preferable for women

Black tie optional:
    if you own a tux, wear it—or a dark suit, white shirt, and formal tie.
    long or short cocktail dress for women

Semiformal:
    dark suit, white shirt, and tie for men
    cocktail dress or dressy fabrics in beautiful styles for women

Cocktail:
    see semiformal

Business attire:
    look like you've come from work

Business casual:
    less dressy form of business (see following section)

Casual dress:
    lean more toward business casual with a jacket or tie you can take off
    for women, most not-too-dressy clothing will work

Casual, but festive:
    casual with fancier fabrics, more colorful, theme motifs

California casual:
    more relaxed than business casual

Barbecue casual:
    Bermudas, aloha shirts, sun dresses probably okay

Resort cocktail:
    washed silks and sandals, gold jewelry, bare shoulders, linen sport jackets

Resort casual:
    upscale, expensive looking Bermudas, cropped pants, sandals

Tourist tacky:
    Beware of this classification. Don't take this literally unless you know your group.

"Barbecue Casual."

INAPPROPRIATE BUSINESS CASUAL

What would erode your credibility, prestige, and professionalism? What is not appropriate business casual attire?

- Anything
  - too tight
  - too young
  - too short
  - too low (no cleavage or hairy chests)
  - too sexy (no underwear showing, no cropped tops)
  - too rumpled
- Anything identified with a category other than your profession
  - Hiking clothes
  - Work-out clothes (sweat suits, jogging suits, bicycle shorts, tennies)
  - Beach clothes
  - Weekend wear (if you'd put it on to go to the store on Saturday, it's probably not the right thing to wear to work.)
- No T-shirts with your favorite beer slogan
- Be careful with
  - bare legs
  - sandals (no toed hose)
  - jeans (be sure they look new)

Alaska to New York. It does, however, imply comfort. Khakis or Dockers, not pressed gabardines. Hush puppies or walkers, not oxfords or spiked heels. Sport coat, not suit coat; chambray shirt, maybe no tie, maybe no jacket. Even a great aloha shirt, but always a classy "I can do the job" appearance.

The confusion in the workplace has a lot to do with people jumping on to the word "casual" without remembering the "business" modifier. Business casual still must mean "dress for success," not "dress for recess."

Four categories of dress which might clarify the situation:

Business formal
Business casual
Everyday casual
Uniforms

We know that business formal is the suit. Suits are economical. Most people look better in suits than in any other kind of clothing. We know what uniforms are, and we may feel lucky if we get to wear one: no need to think about what to wear. Maybe we don't

APPROPRIATE BUSINESS CASUAL

▸ Jackets that are as comfortable as sweaters: those made of modern stretch materials. Some eliminate the buttons and leave off the collar.

▸ Lab coats that can double as overcoats

▸ Knit shirts or quality T-shirts under jackets

▸ Blouses with spandex for comfort, not tightness

▸ Zipfront tops

▸ Pant suits for women, unmatched being more casual than matched

▸ Executive suits in more casual fabrics and worn with relaxed shirts and shoes

▸ Sweater sets

▸ Cardigans as jacket substitutes

▸ Quality catalogue-basic clothing with investment accessories, such as leather boots, crocodile belt, distinctive satchel or tote. A key to not appearing overly casual is the quality of the clothing and the accessories.

▸ "With-it" styles in conservative colors

▸ Conservative styles in "with-it" colors

▸ Doing a little bit more of the unexpected, but not the shocking: bright-colored braces, playful earrings

▸ Clothes with more flair

▸ Clothes that are more playful

▸ Clothing that looks upper middle class: simple, classic, neutral or monochromatic color combos, quality

▸ Solid colors (with prints remember, vertical stripes give authority, curved lines are more playful, and meandering patterns may not be going anywhere.)

▸ Cropped or skinny pants can update a women's suit

▸ Long, loose, flowing skirts

▸ Loafers, slip-ons, wedgies

▸ Casual button-down oxford shirts, not dress shirts

▸ Classic sweater that is not too tight, perhaps topped with a cardigan

▸ Borrowed looks from the golf course: fine-knit polo style shirts, microfiber trousers, but not the spiked shoes

▸ Soft fabrics can be used in structured garments

know the difference between everyday casual and business casual. Everyday casual is what you'd wear around the house or to run to the store. It is important to distinguish this from business casual.

In business casual, the same rules of appropriateness, grooming, fit, and quality apply as when we dress more formally, but the emphasis is on comfort. Companies that implement "business casual"

Always have a jacket handy.

policies do so because they believe that when you are more comfortable, your productivity and morale goes up. But it is also important that your credibility, prestige, and professionalism remain high.

Remember, business casual dressing is for serious business. Look in the mirror before you leave in the morning and ask yourself, "Am I dressing down a little too much?" or, "Would I buy a used car from this person?"

If you are uncertain how to dress, take a cue from your boss. Remember to always have a jacket handy. Keep one at the office for impromptu meetings with clients. Finally, you can always call ahead to find out the dress code at a client's office. It's better to be overdressed than underdressed. You can always take off the jacket. When you match your clients expectations, you put them at ease.

Use what you have learned in this chapter to complete the chart, "Dress to Enhance Your Credibility." Compare your answers with those at the bottom of the chart. How much have you already learned?

● ●

Dress to enhance your credibility

1. Dress for the job you w _ _ _, not the job you h _ _ _.

2. Dress in q _ _ _ _ _ _ clothing and carry q _ _ _ _ _ _ props.

3. Dress c _ _ _ _ _ _ _ _ _ _ so you can work and move easily.

4. Dress professionally, _ _ _ _ _ _ _ _ _ _ _ _ (occasionally, once a month, consistently).

5. Dress to be _ _ cluded, not _ _ cluded.

6. Dress using accessories that carry the eye to your _ _ _ _.

7. Dress in clothing that allows people to notice y _ _, not your

   c _ _ _ _ _ _ _.

8. Dress self-_ _ _ _ _ _ _ _ _ _ , not self- _ _ _ _ _ _ _ _ _ _ _.

9. Dress for the d _ _ at hand.

10. Dress casually in a _ _ _ _ _ _ _, _ _ _ _ _ manner.

11. Dress to sell yourself in the first i _ _ _ _ _ _ _ _ _.

12. Dress carefully, paying attention to the d _ _ _ _ _ _.

Answers: 1. want, have 2. quality, quality 3. comfortably 4. consistently 5. in, ex 6. face 7. you, clothing 8. confidently, consciously 9. day 10. precise, exact 11. impression 12. details

THE INVITATION SAYS "BUSINESS CASUAL"

Below are three different business casual scenarios. Each includes a list of what not to wear and what will fill the bill. As you look at the business casual suggestions, remember that all items must be good quality, in good repair, and fit with ease.

SITUATION #1: A WEEKEND RETREAT AT A CALIFORNIA GOLF RESORT

DON'T WEAR	WEAR
jeans	khaki or light colored trousers
tight shirt	polo shirt
exposed body piercing	turtleneck
shoes with spike heels	slip on shoes
wing tip shoes	walking shoes
hiking boots	golf shoes (spikeless)
flip-flops	leather sandals
T-shirt (with logo)	pullover or cardigan
short shorts	walking or Bermuda shorts
tailored suit	cropped pants
excessive or flashy jewelry	quality golf jacket
unnatural makeup	sport jacket
tie	aloha shirt

How casual is business casual?

SITUATION #2: A WINTER HOLIDAY PARTY IN OMAHA, NEBRASKA

DON'T WEAR	WEAR
low-cut glitzy gown	silk or satin shirt
revealing shirt	ankle length skirt
tie (unless holiday theme)	velvet pants
holiday T-shirt	holiday sweater
sweats (or holiday sweatshirt)	quality sport shirt
ski jacket	sport jacket
matched suit	braces with holiday tie
jeans	corduroy, wool, or microfiber pants
galoshes	leather boots
wing tip shoes	holiday socks
denim jacket	simple quality dress with flats
polar fleece	jewel tones
all your holiday accessories at once	add a touch of whimsy

continued

Where is the business in business casual?

All casual is not business casual.

THE INVITATION SAYS "BUSINESS CASUAL"

SITUATION #3: A SATURDAY BUSINESS MEETING IN NEW YORK CITY

DON'T WEAR	WEAR
tailored business suit	sport coat
jeans	microfiber or gabardine pants
denim jacket	unconstucted jacket
hiking clothes	optional tie (should be playful)
sweats	sweaters
excessive glitz	beautiful scarf, casual jewelry
polar fleece jacket	pullover or cardigan sweater
low-cut or revealing shirt	knit top, turtleneck
T-shirt (with logo)	casual suit: knit, corduroy, suede
flowery prints	dark tones
shoes with spike heels	slip-on shoes
wing tip shoes	leather boots
tennis shoes	good walking shoes

We're talking about form over substance, and this may be making you uncomfortable. We're sure you will agree that an effective appearance will never be a substitute for ability. But you certainly don't want the way you look to be an obstacle to people's evaluation of your performance. You want to be able to get in the door and show people how competent you really are!

review

What do you remember about this chapter that is significant to *you*? First list surprises, "ahas," lightbulbs in the page of your journal that follows. Then, look back through this chapter and list those discoveries you want to highlight.

● ● ● ● ● ● ● ● ● ● ● ● ● ● ● ● ● ● ● ●

Review: chapter 3

"Ahas"

1. _____

_____

2. _____

_____

3. _____

_____

Discoveries to highlight

_____

_____

_____

_____

_____

_____

The review page at the end of this chapter will be useful later as you want to review *Dress Smart*. You won't need to reread the chapter, just your "ahas."

evolutionize your look

4

It is inevitable that we all will age. Our once-taut skin will soften and fill with lines. Along with the development of a wise face can come greater and greater style. The secret is to become more aware of yourself and what makes you *you*.

As E. E. Cummings said,

> To be nobody but yourself in a world which is doing its best, night and day, to make you everybody else means to fight the hardest battle which any human being can fight, and never stop fighting.

relaxation exercise

Now is the time for you to visualize the authentic, ideal YOU. The following relaxation exercise was written by Kerstin VanDervoort, a "Wordsworker," friend, and associate. It will work best if you record it and play it to yourself *or* have someone read it while you experience it.

We'll do a relaxation exercise that can accomplish three objectives:

1. It can help you come from where you have been to be "here" now.
2. It can give you the physiological and psychological benefits of a healthful nap.
3. It can provide some valuable information about your own style choices *and* set you on a positive track toward your best.

We'll ask you to relax, breathe, close your eyes and daydream yourself looking and feeling great. This day is going to be *perfect*. In this daydream, dream big and then dream bigger. Exercise your highest hopes, your wildest wants, your deepest dreams.

This day is *not* a once in a lifetime day, *not* a special vacation day, *not* the day after you win the lottery day. This is a regular, ordinary, normal day in AN IDEAL LIFE. This day will be a nice, regular day in a LIFETIME that your ideal you is living—a life led by you as genius, great talent, creative person with unlimited resources. Again, a normal day, but in a life designed for you to fully bloom.

You will want to be ready to jot down some notes after we're finished. Have a pen all set before we begin. Turn now to the journal pages and be ready to make these notes.

▶ As you exhale, gently let yourself sink down deeper, further, into more comfortable relaxation.
▶ You are moving nowhere, at ease with yourself.
▶ Breathe in deep and long.
▶ See the number one in your mind three times.
▶ Exhale naturally and easily and let yourself go. . . .

You are noise free, like a still, clear lake. Now,

▶ Let your breathing happen just as it wants to . . .
▶ Let your attention withdraw, gently, from any distractions
▶ Just be here now.

If you feel restless or uncomfortable at any time, just try another full, deep breath, floating out the distraction with your exhalation. You are about to bring into your mind an ideal, substance-of-your-everyday-life-as-you'd-love-to-live-it, as you'd-love-it-to-be, situation.

▶ Let your imagination have a field day.
▶ Let yourself create an "ordinary-everyday" day of your most ideal life.

Dream this day to make it just perfect for you. Create the most harmonious, beautiful, absolutely appropriate scenes for your own unique wants, personality, and dreams.

In a few moments, you'll be opening an imaginary door to look into an imaginary mirror. In a few moments, you'll see how you are dressed, how you look, in this ordinary day of an ideal life.

Right now, see the door and let it appear to you in detail, and prepare yourself to look your most attractive, most healthy, most capable, most confident, most talented, most pleasing self. You'll be noticing what you are wearing and how you feel and look. You are about to gaze into a mirror that reflects back your best, deepest, highest self.

▶ Ready . . . breathe . . . open the door.
▶ Look at yourself, and as you look, notice what textures, fabrics, colors, and style you are wearing to feel perfectly comfortable, to look perfectly matched to who you are.
▶ Make any changes, improvements, or adjustments you want to make your image even *better*.
▶ Observe and note what feels completely beautiful and completely appropriate to you—cotton? linen? wool? silk? leather? What colors? patterns? weights? textures?
▶ Notice what's on your feet . . . what accessories you have . . . look at your skin, eyes, hair.
▶ How do you stand? How do you move?

See everything with complete confidence that what you are wearing and how you look is a perfect expression of your best self today. As you look at yourself, at the picture you've created to feel right about, to enjoy, become aware of how you feel physically on this particular day in your ideal life. How is your balance, your weight distribution? How do you feel in your clothes, your shoes, your jewelry, watch, accessories?

Now observe yourself calmly, with full attention, remembering that this particular mirror shows you at your best and helps you remember that imagining *how* you want to be, look, and feel is the crucial step to being, looking, and feeling that way.

Look into your own face in your mirror now and create the expression,

the eyes,
the demeanor,

that express you at full ease, and confident that you are completely comfortable in your body . . . radiating willingness to energize your most cherished capacities fully.

- ► Enjoy seeing what you see.
- ► Give yourself a moment, now, to savor even more fully this ideal person you see.
- ► Enjoy.
- ► Thank yourself and your imagination for entertaining you so well.
- ► Just rest into that nice warm glow of gratitude for now.

When you feel ready, begin to come back, stir and move gently. Open your eyes feeling energized for continuing, refreshed and renewed, aware of your unlimited possibilities, highest hopes, wildest wants, deepest dreams, and most cherished strengths, all of which are *clues* to you of your potential.

This would be a good time to jot down very quickly just some random words, phrases, images that occur to you from the scene you just played. Even quick sketches will help give you access to this information later.

● ●

Notes on relaxation exercise

_____

_____

_____

_____

_____

_____

_____

_____

_____

_____

_____

_____

_____

_____

_____

_____

_____

_____

_____

_____

_____

_____

_____

_____

_____

_____

_____

_____

_____

_____

_____

_____

_____

_____

_____

_____

_____

_____

_____

_____

You can't have *style* if you are a slave to fashion.

what is style anyway?

Style is the totality of your self-projection. It includes your personality, clothes, haircut, and image. It is the way you walk and talk. Your style sets you apart from others and makes you unique. Having style is not the same as being stylish, for the stylish person is fashionable. Style is different from fashion because fashion is changeable; it is dictated by trends and fads. You can take pieces of fashion and make them part of your style, but you can't have style while being a slave to fashion.

What is *your* style? Is it as you would like it to be? Is it perceived similarly by you and others? Do you fit into any categories? You need to understand yourself to develop style, and you need to be aware that the way you perceive yourself may differ from the way others perceive you. Only you know how you *want* to be perceived.

Do you and your friends agree on the image
you are projecting?

Let's look back at questions 3 and 4 in Chapter 1 (women) and Chapter 2 (men). What words did you check to describe yourself? Most of these words appear in the "Style words" chart. Place a check in the "me" column next to those words that you checked in the questionnaire. Then, compare your self-perceptions of your style with those of two friends. Ask them to look at the word lists and check the words in the chart that describe your style. You will want to cover the columns that the friend is not marking.

Do you and your friends agree on the style you are projecting? Or, are their perceptions different from yours? Why do you differ? Write your conclusions about these discussions in the "Observations" section below the chart.

Then, list all the words you circled in questions 3 and 4 on the questionnaire in the "Comparison" section of the journal pages that follow. Star those that you both marked and circled. Do any of them match perceptions you or others already have of you? Underline those. They're the easiest ones!

● ● ● ● ● ● ● ● ● ● ● ● ● ● ● ● ● ●

Style words

Example (check what applies):	Friend #2	Friend #1	Me
sophisticated			
romantic			
sensuous			
preppy			
tailored			
understated, quality			

continued

Style words (*continued*)

Example (check what applies):	*Friend #2*	*Friend #1*	*Me*
regal			
authoritative			
severe			
individualistic			
casual, sporty			
earthy			
smart, but not trendy			
classic, with flair			
tweedy			
clothing as art			
international, ethnic			
neutral and natural			
clean and simple			
conservative			

continued

Style words (continued)

Example (check what applies):	Friend #2	Friend #1	Me
elegant			
"my only limitation is my imagination"			
Western			
dramatic			
fashionable			
confident			
stylish			
at ease			
energetic			
enthusiastic			
robust			
determined			
feminine			
masculine			

continued

Style words (*continued*)

Example (check what applies):	*Friend #2*	*Friend #1*	*Me*
successful			
tasteful			
crisp and clean			
comfortable			
detailed, accessorized, finished			
matching, coordinated			
colorful			
unusual, unique			
professional			
inattentive to detail			
perky, fresh			
carefree			
careless			
couldn't care less about clothes			

●●●●●●●●●●●●●●●●●●●●●●●●

Observations

_____

_____

_____

_____

_____

_____

_____

_____

●●●●●●●●●●●●●●●●●●●●●●●●

Comparison

_____

_____

_____

_____

_____

_____

_____

_____

_____

_____

●●●●●●●●●●●●●●●●●●●●●●●●

Are you being realistic about how you would like to look?

Now, for the impossible. Are you being realistic about how you would like to look? For instance, are you large-boned and statuesque in build and want to look dainty? Or, are there a few ways you would like to look, but could never possibly manage. Go back and scratch out those impossible-for-you style words. The rest you can work on!

ingredients of style

Have you ever cooked dinner from a nearly bare cupboard? If you have only a few food items from which to choose, you tend to be more creative with how you combine them. The same applies to you and your clothing. This is the first of many times we will mention the need to limit your wardrobe, the need to simplify your life by having fewer items from which to choose. By breaking habits and trying new combinations of a few wonderful clothing items, you will refine your style and feel good about stretching and expanding the creative person within you.

So, what would your special clothing be like, those items that make you look and feel terrific? They would not be decorative or ex-aggerated or contrived, but honestly reflect you. They would look comfortable and efficient and not indicate you tried too hard. They would be pleasing to the eye *and* functional. These special clothes would enhance your coloring, lifestyle, figure, values, tastes, and age. They would be appropriate to the occasion, both to the activity and to the event. The clothing items would exude quality: quality of design, quality of fabric, quality of workmanship. No puckered shoulders or misshapen seams. Everything would appear genuine and expensive. No junk!

You don't need *a lot* of clothes, but what you do own must be wonderful. Have you ever been in a nearly empty room which was very tastefully done? You probably noticed what was there, not what was missing. The same principle applies to your clothing. It will not be noticed if you are not wearing a belt as long as your skirt and blouse are fabulous. So when you do get around to buying that belt, make it as special as the other clothing you own. Then it will be an-other in your cadre of quality possessions.

And those friendly clothes will fit and look at ease on your body—nothing too small or too large. Your clothing will work together eas-ily. There will be good balance and symmetry and proportion. Peo-ple of taste put quality things together well, but not just because they match. When you dress, you are creating a piece of art. You are the canvas, and every piece you add is another element of the whole. Use your full-length mirror to practice restraint and know when to stop adding. Less *is* more. You don't want the eye to jump around. One focal point or point of interest is often enough. In terms of design, uneven quantities are more appealing than even quanti-ties. Don't use two, four, or six details. The emphasis can be a spe-cial pin on your lapel, a wonderful tie, or a spot of color peeking from your pocket. You want people to zero in on something indi-

Pay attention to quality and detail. Nothing at all is better than junk.

vidual, something that is you, something that gives you flair or panache. That something is your signature. Think about what jewelry or clothing you could not lend because it would be noticed to be yours. You may not have a personal signature yet, but it is worth watching for as you move through life.

A person with style is consistent in dress. There is a direction, a continuity, an evolutionary insight. Change is good for us all, but minimal change in our look indicates we are stable and shows that we know ourselves; we are discerning and able to make good choices. We learn to select the best of everything available and use it to our advantage. To have style, we must have taste and know excellence.

A person with style has a sense of humor. As Yves St. Laurent says, our outfits can show a mixture of "serious and giggle." How about wearing that special pin on your hem or wearing a tie whose overall pattern is a performing symphony?

Pay attention to details. Nothing must be out of place. For example, inappropriate earrings are worse than no earrings at all! Beautifully manicured nails are stylish, but it is far better to wear no polish than to have what you are wearing chipped. Most underwear is meant to stay under. You need a full-length mirror to attend to every detail when you dress each morning.

begin creating your personal style

Some people seem to be born with style, but most people develop it by being curious and aware. It is comforting to know that style has nothing to do with looks. Some of the most "gorgeous" people have developed no individual look. And some very plain faces are full of stylish character. Style is an attitude, a self-confidence, and a statement about you, the unique, wonderful, individual that you are.

How can you develop your personal style? Well, the first step is by just being aware of the ingredients and determining what you like and dislike. Therefore, first complete three comparisons: (1) style elements you find positive and negative, (2) people whose styles you like or dislike, and (3) fashion illustrations you find attractive or unattractive.

Complete the chart on journal page 100 that compares the words that are positive style ingredients (e.g., quality, discernment, ease, point of emphasis) with those that are style poisonous (e.g., too small, too dowdy, too overmatched).

Some people seem to be born with style, but *most* people develop it.

Then, go a bit further and carefully observe people you consider to have style. Whose style do you admire? This could be a person you know or someone you know of, such as Grace Kelly, Queen Latifah, Hillary Clinton, Clint Eastwood, Hugh Grant, George W. Bush. How have they dressed? What is it you like about their image? The next time you see this person, "stand still and look until you really see." Does she always wear pearls, even when they are tucked under her collar and are nondiscernible to most people? Does he have a unique, yet classic, hair style? Wear cowboy boots? What is the signature? List your observations under "People with Style."

Now, observe people who have no style, no class, no flair. List these people and the qualities that they possess that make you put them in such a category (e.g., chews gum, pants to tight, tasteless tattoo). List your observations under "People Without Style." Then, compare the two lists.

Finally, on page 101, compare illustrations in fashion magazines. What kinds of socks are put with what kinds of shoes, and how? What accessories are worn? What layering occurs? How are colors utilized? Be critical. Decide what appeals to you, and figure out why. Clip out pictures of looks you like and ones you dislike. Complete the two charts in your journal, "Fashion Pictures with Style" and "Fashion Pictures Without Style."

Observe other people. Note those who have no style, no class, no flair.

● ●

Comparison 1: key style ingredients

Positive   *Negative*

_____

_____

_____

_____

_____

● ●

Comparison 2: people with and without style

People with Style

Name   Signature

_____

_____

_____

_____

_____

_____

People Without Style

Initials or Name   Qualities Indicating Lack of Style

_____

_____

_____

_____

_____

_____

● ● ● ● ● ● ● ● ● ● ● ● ● ● ● ● ● ● ● ●

Comparison 3: fashion illustrations

Fashion Pictures with Style

_____

_____

_____

_____

_____

_____

_____

_____

_____

_____

Fashion Pictures Without Style

_____

_____

_____

_____

_____

_____

_____

_____

_____

_____

● ● ● ● ● ● ● ● ● ● ● ● ● ● ● ● ● ● ● ●

Next, review your charts and a make a final comparison: style elements you like and style elements you dislike. Note what you have concluded to be the really telling clothing item(s) or personal signature(s). What says "notice me, I have flair. I am an individual and proud of my individuality?" Is it the shoes that are always perfect? Is it the briefcase or purse? Is it the subtle use of jewelry? Is it the fabrics? Is it the consideration, alertness to other's needs and sensitivity? Or can you not isolate any one quality that repeats itself on those people whose style you admire, in the magazines and on the mannequins and personnel at the finer clothing stores? Then, determine what qualities seem "tacky" (e.g., elastic waistband pulling beneath sweater to show bare skin when leaning over). Write your observations in the "Style elements" chart in your journal.

● ●

Comparison 4: style elements

Style Elements You Like

_____

_____

_____

_____

_____

_____

_____

Style Elements You Dislike

_____

_____

_____

_____

_____

_____

_____

● ●

Finally, create a timetable for experimenting with the elements you like and creating your own style. Complete the "Style Development" chart. You will return to it often to evaluate your progress.

● ●

Style development

Style idea	Occasion when I will try it out	Date	Observations

A NOTE ABOUT TRADITIONAL CLASSIFICATION TOOLS

According to *Brain Sex: The Real Difference between Men and Women* by Anne Moir and David Jessel (Dell Publishing, 1992), no matter how we fight it, our brains are programmed by our gender, as are our bodies, for reproduction of our species . . . even though at this point in history over-reproduction has freed us of that focus.

By that paradigm, women are looking for a provider and men are looking for a producer. Women must attract, while men must exhibit the strengths by which they will provide.

The traditional classifications of men and women which we discuss in *Dress Smart* grew out of this view. Women, often today's providers, may want to take a look at the men's quiz and male classifications as well, and to a lesser degree, vice versa.

BASIC STYLES FOR WOMEN

Dramatic
a. Extreme high fashion, long, draped clinging silhouette, severe angular or restrained curved lines; satin, lamé, heavy rich fabrics; black, chartreuse, gold colors, subtle or bold contrasts of color; extreme hats, gloves, shoes

Natural
b. Informal, casual, comfortable clothes, rough textures and natural finishes such as raw silk, shantung, tweeds; emphasis on belts, pockets, buttons for trim; earthy and/or primary colors

Classic
c. Tailored lines, simple, smart, refined, no extremes of fashion, small-scale yang, simplified yin

Romantic
d. Glamorous, extremely feminine fashions, fitted bodice, bouffant skirt, black lace or chiffon, garnet velvet

Gamine
e. Pleated skirts, short jackets, nipped in waists, fitted sweaters, Peter Pan collars, small plaids, downsized "natural" clothing; (See "b" above) "Elfin" look; tunics, tailored pants, boots

Ingenue
f. Rounded silhouette; gathered fullness, boleros, rococo curves, crisp organdy, voile, dotted swiss, soft angora; pastels or clear, sparkling tints

Yin-Yang.

♀ personality-dress-body classifications

There have been a number of personality-dress-body classifications for women done over the years. One of the first was conceived and developed by Belle Northrup. Her Yin-Yang[1] classification places persons into one of six areas based on their feminine or masculine traits. Yin is the feminine and Yang is the masculine. Neither is

The six basic types for women.

better than the other and, in fact, both are necessary to make the whole.

For questions 5–12 in Chapter 1, add up the number of times you chose a, b, c, d, e, and f. The letter you chose most often will indicate the basic style into which you would most likely fit. Match your letter with the category on the previous page, and then check the descriptions about your category in the chart that follows.

Yin–Yang classification

| | Yang | | Intermediate | | Yin | |
	DRAMATIC	NATURAL	CLASSIC	ROMANTIC	GAMINE	INGENUE
Height	Above average	Above average	Average	Average	Below average	Below average
Build	Current fashion figure, angular, large boned, long limbs	Strong, muscular, sturdy, stocky, broad or square shoulders	Average for height, well proportioned	Beautiful, feminine figure, long legged	Small boned, compact, well coordinated	Small boned, dainty, feminine, delicate
Posture	Fashionable or erect, stiff, elevated chin, weight on heels	Relaxed and casual or vigorous and alert; solid, flat heeled; hands on hips	Easily erect, poised, well balanced	Graceful, willowy, relaxed	Alert, perky, hands on hips	Graceful, ballet posture, head tilted, appealing, compliant
Head Contour	Long oval, high cheekbones, flat planes in cheeks, angular	Broad or long, square jaw, wide forehead	Oval	Beautiful, heart shaped, triangular	Small rounded cheeks and chin	Width between eyes, rounded cheeks and chin
Eyes	Deep-set, heavy lids, close together, angled	Average for size, friendly, approachable	Average size, clear, direct gaze	Large, beautiful, melting, long lashed, alluring glance	Wide open, wide apart, twinkling, friendly	Large, round, wide open, long lashes, coy or demure glance
Eyebrows	Sharply defined, angular line	Heavy, dark, natural, straight	Pleasing arch	Arched	Natural	Delicate, natural arch
Nose	Long, pointed, flared nostrils, straight or convex, curved in profile	Strong, large, blunt, heavy, irregular	Straight, well shaped, average size	Delicate, long, straight, or turned up	Short, turned up, rounded, "button end"	Dainty, fine boned, upward tilt
Mouth	Wide, flat curve; thin or heavy lips held firmly	Wide, average or heavy lips, smiling	Well modeled	Curved, full lips, slightly parted	Small, rounded	"Rosebud" or heart shaped, soft, relaxed
Hair Style	Plain, severe, extremes of fashion, center part with chignon is typical	Casual, short, unset, mannish, not fussy	Simple, neat, plain but not severe	Long, curly, soft feminine style	Short, natural, bangs, pony tail, straight or curly	Curly, short, feather cut

continued

Yin–Yang classification *(continued)*

| | Yang | | Intermediate | | Yin | |
	DRAMATIC	NATURAL	CLASSIC	ROMANTIC	GAMINE	INGENUE
Coloring	Definite, extreme contrasts	Natural, outdoor sun-kissed	Medium to light chocolaty, low contrast	Rich and glowing	Natural	Light, fair, chocolate
Hair	Black, dark brown, auburn, bright bleached blonde, henna	Dark, medium brown or auburn, frosted	Light brown, medium blonde, dark, black if dark skin	Dark, golden blonde, red	Light brown to blonde, black	Blonde or brown, black
Skin	Dark, olive, or cream	Tanned, freckled, natural looking	Clear, with no sharp contrasts	Clear, fair, or dark, fine textured	Natural, tanned or freckled	Pink and white or brown, fine textured
Eyes	Black, brown	Dark brown, hazel	Blue or hazel, black or brown	Violet, dark blue, brown or black	Blue, hazel, brown	Blue, dark
Expressive Manner	Formal, dignified, reserved, haughty, sophisticated	Free, easy, frank, open, friendly	Gracious, poised, well mannered, mature, conventional	Flirtatious, charmingly feminine	Direct, natural tomboy	Sparkling, gay, or demure and shy
Voice	Low, husky, resonant, emphatic, deliberate	Naturally low pitch, strong, clear	Well modulated, pleasing	Soft, feminine	Low pitch, boisterous	Soft, gentle, high pitch
Walk and Gestures	Decisive energetic, or slow and purposeful	Long strides, free swinging, large, easy, relaxed, natural	Calm, poised, well controlled	Graceful, languorous	Quick, skipping, free swinging, awkward, natural	Graceful, light, airy
Age	Mature or appears older than others of same age	Friendly and casual at any age	Poised at any age	"Over twenty," but never old	Young or appears so	Youthful or appears young

continued

Yin–Yang classification (continued)

| | Yang | | Intermediate | | Yin | |
	DRAMATIC	NATURAL	CLASSIC	ROMANTIC	GAMINE	INGENUE
Clothing	Extremes, in fashion	Sportswear, boots, leather skirts, sweaters	No extremes; soft, straight lines; immaculately tailored	Feminine styles, bouffant or softly draped, theatrical flair but not extreme, low-cut necklines, fitted waists	Casual, tailored, youthful Preppy-look, small-scale sporty clothing, short jackets, pleated skirts, peter pan collars	Ruffles and bows to be given up eventually, feminine trims and styles, curved lines, fresh, unsophisticated, natural, delicate, dainty
Jewelry	Bold, simple or elaborate, ornate	Simple, minimal	Conservative, average size, quality	Delicate	Classic, little-boy utilitarian	Delicate, dainty
Makeup	Exaggerated	Minimal	Conservative	Strong but not overdone, fake eyelashes	Minimal, natural	Pink lips, pink cheeks, doll-like
Fabrics and Textures	Severely plain or lavishly ornate, bold, vivid, wild prints, shiny, glittery	Tweeds, checks, paisleys, plaids, large, casual prints, nubby, handwoven, natural fabrics	High-quality fabrics, shiny or matte, cottons, jerseys, wools, knits, qiana, silks, small to medium prints, traditional designs, polka dots, paisley	Soft and luxurious, sheer, rounded prints	Small-scale plaids, ginghams, checks, crisp cottons, wools	Soft silks, delicate floral prints, lightweight fabrics, matte finish, softly flowing
Evening	Satin, crepe, heavy brocade, metallic, theatrical or striking	Matte finish, crepe, raw silk, jersey, quilted materials	Chiffon, silk, tissue fabric, brocade, not rough	Chiffon, velvet, silks, lace, satin, brocade	Fabrics with body: raw silk, jersey, linen; classic dressed-up styles, matte finish	Voile, organdy, dotted swiss, lightweight jersey, youthful feminine fabrics, nothing heavy or dramatic

♂ classifications for men

Men do not fit into the Yin-Yang classifications, but rather into one
of Charles Hix's[2] basic styles:

a. The Connoisseur
b. The Drum Major
c. The Moderator
d. The Solid Citizen
e. The Good Scout

The five basic types for men.

THE FIVE BASIC STYLES

a. **The Connoisseur.** You are the man who always exhibits impeccable, "classy" taste. Your clothing spells out Q-U-A-L-I-T-Y and A-S-S-U-R-A-N-C-E. You move self-confidently with your clothing, it's an extension of you. You are always well appointed, with a marked tendency to dress on the formal side. When your clothing is carefully accessorized (with gold collar pins and silk pocket squares, for example), you appear urbane, well traveled, perhaps monied, even aristocratic. (In a pared-down version, with minimal accessories, you represent a cool and reserved authority figure but may shed the world-traveling, gentle side of your persona.) However, if the look is carried to an extreme, you can become the dilettante. One cardinal rule in dressing is: Nothing impedes like excess.

b. **The Drum Major.** You lead the parade in what onlookers see as "in" apparel. Although you are inclined to be adventurous, your appearance is not brash. You stand out from the crowd because many crowd members simply recede into anonymity. Your well-thought-out clothing choices, selected from new trends in advance of the general population, exemplify your consciousness of what you're wearing. Because you want to dress equally fashionably and tastefully, the astute observer may not consider you to be as free thinking as you would like, particularly if you fail to individualize your wardrobe with an ongoing personal stamp. However, when trendiness is tempered with insight, your wardrobe is characterized by extraordinary flair. On the other hand, when you go overboard and wear only mouth-opening conversation-stopping clothes, you are transformed into the Brass Band, a caricature of fashion. At these times, you're not only a victim of fashion; you're fashion's fatality.

c. **The Moderator.** You dress handsomely but in an elusive manner. Perhaps the best description is "eclectic" because your style is not iron clad. You are predictable only to the extent that you are invariably well groomed and somewhat understated. You don't demand the spotlight, although the others may naturally gravitate to you. Your clothing is always artfully conceived for an unpremeditated look. Unfortunately, it's easy to execute this style poorly. If you make the error of perfectly matching the color of your necktie to the hue of your breast handkerchief, for instance, you no longer look spontaneous but studied. Then instead of coming across as the Moderator, you assume the guise of the Manipulator.

d. **The Solid Citizen.** You dress conventionally, some might say almost monotonously. But what your clothing lacks in imagination, it makes up for in "correctness." You are never flashy, but you aren't necessarily dull. Although your wardrobe tends to be interchangeable with your peers' wardrobes, you look like a man who is trustworthy and clearheaded. Occasionally, you may introduce a fillip of innovation, but on a minor (never a major) note. When you slavishly follow the dress-to-succeed dictates, however, your clothing becomes a uniform to proclaim your membership in a privileged caste. When you start judging other men only on the basis of how closely they dress in your mold, you are no longer a Solid Citizen, but a Vigilante.

e. **The Good Scout.** You are always casually dressed; not sloppily, not thoughtlessly, but casually. You dislike pretensions in attire; you eschew anything flamboyant. How you dress is a reflection of your fashion philosophy. You are a true democrat in your conviction that clothing should never establish barriers between people. You wear garments because they are comfortable, not to impress. But you are always neat. You stand for reliability. But should you ever become haphazard in your self-presentation, or you run the risk of being mistaken for the Hick.

For questions 5–19 in Chapter 2, add up the number of times you chose a, b, c, d, and e. The letter you chose most often will indicate the basic style into which you most likely fit. Match your letter with the category above, and then check the descriptions about your category in the table that follows.

Styles to suit your type

	CONNOISSEUR	DRUM MAJOR	MODERATOR	SOLID CITIZEN	GOOD SCOUT
SUIT	Custom made, not trendy, well cut, somber color, smooth fabric, maybe vested	Grey flannel or dark camel, fashion oriented	Understated elegance associated with British tailoring, untraditional touches, gray flannel, heathered	Conformist, pin stripe, single breasted	Comfortable loose fit, traditional blue and camel, flannel and tweed
SPORTS JACKET	For country or country club, not for business, dark toned with gray or navy pants	Tweedy texture, small checks, unusual colorations	Beefy fabrics, definite patterns, country touches (i.e., leather, horn buttons)	No "big splashes": single-breasted navy or camel blazer	Nubby herringbone, muted plaid, hop-sacking, raw silk, homespun wools and tweeds
DRESS SHIRT AND TIE	Broadcloth, white, white collar, French cuff, authoritative pin stripe, repp tie, small-scale pattern, no plaids	Matching shirt and tie, dark shirt and light tie, collarless and tieless, current fashion	Oxford and broadcloth, subtle stripes or tattersall checks, small pattern tie: paisley, geometric	Solid color button-downs, various checks in sedate colors; Repp-stripe, paisley or foulard tie	Chambray shirt, striped or plain oxford cloth, button-down, placket front, tie only if necessary
DRESS SHOE	Seamless black leather, highly polished	Tannish oxford adaptation	Not too heavy, wing tips, brownish color	Plain oxford lace-up, nothing bulky	Tasseled slip-on
ACCESSORIES	Minimal jewelry, no pinky rings or tie clasps, small tasteful two-sided cufflinks, silk pocket square, felt formal hat	No flashy rings, no tie tacks, occasional collar pins	Vests, pocket squares, collar pins, not "too much"	Minimal jewelry, practical hat	Not dressy, woven leather belt
OVERCOAT	Navy blue cashmere chesterfield, white silk scarf	Wraparound style, nubby fabric, deep off-brown shade, knotted (not buckled) belt, textured or patterned muffler	Countrified dress coat, balmacaan, rough woolen tweed, maroon flannel scarf reverses to silk foulard	Camel-colored polo coat, neutral scarf	Fly-front trench, removable lining, soft herringbone flannel scarf

continued

Styles to suit your type *(continued)*

	CONNOISSEUR	DRUM MAJOR	MODERATOR	SOLID CITIZEN	GOOD SCOUT
SWEATER	Unadorned V-neck pullover, traditional V-neck cardigan, dark color	Colorful boat neck, V-neck, crew neck or rolled collar, mottled or patterned	Shawl collar, cable stitched, V-neck, crew neck, shetland wool, pullover or cardigan style	Turtleneck, crew, or cardigan in plain basic colors; woven design	Crewneck, sense of heritage, handmade look, fisherman styling and weave
CASUAL SHOE	Well-polished laced shoe	City sandal without socks, sporty cap-toe in light leather	Top-Siders, brown suede, low contrast saddle shoe	Jogging shoe, penny loafer	Hiking shoe, brogue, or moccasin
SPORTS SHIRT	Tattersall check or oxford cloth button down	New and novel, yet tasteful, one shirt over another	Tradition with a twist, tartan plaid	Various knit pullovers, button-down dress shirts, plaids, and flannels	Soft corduroy or flannel, soft neutrals, not trendy color combinations
SLACKS	No beltless styles; moderate belt loops; black, navy, or brown; smooth leather belt	Atypical styles, diversity, jeans, chinos, cords, "with-it" belt or unbelted	Basic color, traditional corduroy, chinos, poplins, traditional belt with signature buckle	Chinos, poplins, gabardines, corduroys; webbed or woven belt	Chino, khaki, corduroy, twill; brown leather belt
WALK SHORTS	Bermuda length, dark colors	Cuffed shortish shorts or medium- to upper thigh-length	Simple solid colors	Standard length, tan	Cargo pockets, tunnel loops
OUTERWEAR	Shortened version of overcoat, Tyrolean hat, navy scarf	Bomber length, fashion color	Nautical-inspired casual jacket	Practicality, serviceability: car coat, parka	Duffle coat with toggle closure, windbreaker
RAINWEAR	Fly-front raincoat, black umbrella	Featherweight glazed cotton, not classic trench, bold striped umbrella	Yoked trench coat, subtly striped umbrella	Utility: streamlined trench coat with epaulettes	Slicker, small collapsible umbrella

summary

It is orderly and neat to find categories for the various parts of our lives. It helps us feel secure to have classifications into which we can slip our actions, our personalities, and our colors. It is comforting to know or to think that something happened to us because we are an Aries, for example. It makes sense of the millions of colors that exist to be told you can wear twenty-eight because you are a "Summer." But we must remember that categories are artificial and because no two people are alike, no person can be accurately and perfectly categorized. You may be a part of more than one classification, or you may not find your place in any of the style categories. Categorization is simply another way of looking at yourself. It is a way of recognizing why you feel uncomfortable in pearls, for example, if you are basically a dramatic person, or why you feel uncomfortable in cords and tweeds if you are a connoisseur.

It is exciting to identify your style, to develop it, to enjoy it, and to grow with it. As you age, you will gradually perfect and refine your style. It will mature with you. Dr. Leopold Bellak and Samm Sinclair Baker say in their book, *Reading Faces:*

> Infants have smooth faces—nearly clean except for their innate characteristics. As we grow older, our face increasingly shows character, a much admired quality. An adult with a "baby face" often is considered bland and uninteresting, immature, and lacking wisdom—he has not lived. A person who has lived an absorbing, creative, worthwhile life has this fact stamped on his face.[3]

We have a great deal to look forward to!

review

What do you remember about this chapter that is significant to *you?* First, list surprises, "ahas," lightbulbs in the page of your journal that follows. Then, look back through this chapter and list those discoveries you want to highlight.

● ●

Review: chapter 4

"Ahas"

1. _____

_____

2. _____

_____

3. _____

_____

Discoveries to highlight

_____

_____

_____

_____

_____

_____

The review page at the end of this chapter will be useful later as you want to review *Dress Smart*. You won't need to reread the chapter, just your "ahas."

endnotes

1. H. T. McJimsey, *Art in Clothing Selection*, Iowa University Press, 1963, pp. 72–74.
2. Reprinted from *How to Dress Your Man* by Charles Hix, Copyright © 1981 by Charles Hix, Crown Publishers, Inc.
3. Dr. Leopold Bellak and Samm Sinclair Baker, *Reading Faces*, Curtis Brown Ltd., 1985.

enrich your raw materials

5

As we discuss your body's assets and proportion, three concepts are basic. If you can tune into them now and keep coming back to them as we continue through this chapter, you will find them comfortable handles to grasp as you work to enrich your raw materials. These concepts are (1) balance, (2) line, and (3) emphasis.

Let's discuss them briefly now and come back to them again and again:

1. BALANCE. Parts of you that are too small in relationship to other parts can look in proportion if you *add* to the too small parts to balance the too large. For example, if your hips are big in proportion to your torso, add shoulder pads to your jacket.
2. LINE. Use lines to bring the eye to your positive features and avoid lines that bring the eye to features you wish to play down. Lines can be stripes, slits, seams, jacket edges, hemlines, cuffs, rick-rack, topstitching, front bands, tucks, gathers, pleats, yokes, buttons, jewelry, scarves. For example, a vertically tucked dress will carry the eye along the tucks from the hem to the neck and add to your height.
3. EMPHASIS. Accents stop the eye. Placing a contrasting color, texture, or detail at a point you wish to emphasize will stop the eye at the asset. For example, pearls at the neck of a black dress will bring the eye upward to the neck and face.

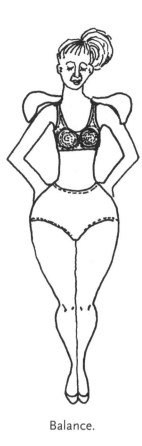

Balance.

Line.

Emphasis.

♀ body measurements

Go back to Chapter 1, questions 38 and 39. Did you barely have any-thing to list as body assets, but needed another sheet to list your faults? Women can be terrible to themselves! The negative self-im-age so many of us have stems from all the perfect-looking bodies we see on television and in magazines. Remember—the photogra-phers know how to show *only* the models' best features. So let's learn to emphasize our positive body parts too! We can minimize our faults by taking our minds off them and thinking instead of our assets. What we want to do is decide what parts of our body are our favorites. Let's call these our Primary Assets and work to bring the eye to these Primary Assets.

The following exercise is very analytical. If you're not in the mood, skip it for now! Come back when you feel ready. Or, if you feel you know your body well enough already, and you know what you want to emphasize, skip this section altogether and go to "Clothing Tricks" on page 135.

Women are often terrible to themselves.

Ask a friend to help you discover your body silhouette.

For those who are up for it, let's get measuring. Find a friend and the following materials: paper to cover a door, masking tape, pencil, tape measure, large magic marker, and yardstick. First let's take your measurements and discover your body silhouette. Complete the three measurement charts in your journal.

● ●

Vertical measurements and body silhouette

▶ Cover a door with paper. Be certain the paper touches the floor.

▶ Wear snug clothing (e.g., leotard, swimsuit) and no shoes.

▶ On one side of the paper, stand sideways with your arm
   nearest the door raised toward the ceiling. Have your friend
   trace your profile view. Be certain to hold the pencil
   perpendicular to the paper.

▶ Stand to the other side of the paper with your back against the
   paper and your feet together. Have your friend trace you.

▶ Have your friend draw a line on the paper at each of the
   following places:

   ▶ 1. Top of head _____

   ▶ 2. Chin _____

   ▶ 3. Neck (base of neck hollow) _____

   ▶ 4. Shoulder: right _____ left _____

   ▶ 5. Armpit: right _____ left _____

   ▶ 6. Nipple: right _____ left _____

   ▶ 7. Elbow: right _____ left _____

   ▶ 8. Waist _____

   ▶ 9. Hipbone: right _____ left _____

   ▶ 10. Thigh joint: right _____ left _____

   ▶ 11. Wrist: right _____ left _____

   ▶ 12. Mid-thigh: right _____ left _____

   ▶ 13. Middle fingertip: right _____ left _____

   ▶ 14. Knee: right _____ left _____

   ▶ 15. And, unless the bottom of the paper is even with the
        floor, draw a line at the floor.

● ● ● ● ● ● ● ● ● ● ● ● ● ● ● ● ● ● ● ●

Circumferential measurements

▶ Measure the following circumferences (distances around) and
   record the inches on the appropriate blank. Do not pull the
   tape too tightly.

▶ 1. Neck _____

▶ 2. Shoulder _____

▶ 3. Waist (you may want to put on a belt to locate precisely your waist) _____

▶ 4. Hip (measure the greatest circumference) _____

▶ 5. Wrist (measure between the wrist bone and the hand, at the wrist joint) _____

▶ 6. Bust (measure over the largest part; keep the tape over the shoulder blades in the back) _____

▶ 7. Calf (measure the greatest circumference) _____

▶ 8. Ankle (measure immediately above the anklebone) _____

● ●

Additional measurements

▶ Measure with the tape and record the following measurements in the blank provided:

▶ 1. Waist to bottom of derriere: right _____ left _____

▶ 2. Inner corner eye to outer corner eye: right _____ left

_____

▶ 3. Inner corner left eye to inner corner right eye _____

▶ 4. Right to left shoulder _____

▶ 5. Neck to waist _____

● ●

♀ your body proportions

You're now ready to place your measurements on the following body proportion chart and interpret where you are off and on. Follow the steps below to complete the "Body Proportion Chart."

1. Measure from the floor-line up to each of the marks on the "Vertical Measurements and Body Silhouette" chart and write the number of inches in the blanks.
2. When applicable, average the right- and left-side measurements and record the average beside each measurement.
3. Using the vertical, circumferential, and additional measurements from the three sections above, fill in your measurements on the following chart.
4. Unless stated otherwise, the distance used in the following chart is the distance from the body part indicated to the floor.
5. After you have recorded your measurements, compare them with your "ideal" measurements and note your conclusions on the Body Proportion Chart.

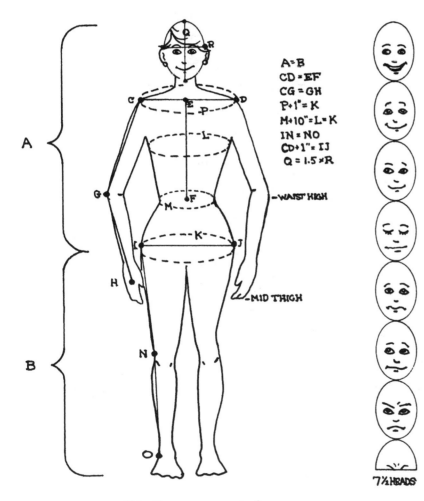

"Ideal" measurements for women.

● ●

Body proportion chart

My Measurements		Ideal Measurements	Conclusions

1. Top of head   a. _____
     Hip   b. _____
     Subtract b from a   c. _____
		Distance from hip to top of head would equal distance from hip to feet. (Line 1b would equal line 1c.)	If c is greater than b, I am long waisted and/or short legged. If b is greater than c, I am short waisted and/or long legged.

2. Thigh joint   a. _____
     Knee   b. _____
     Subtract b from a   c. _____
		Knee would evenly divide leg. (Line 2b would equal line 2c.)	If c is greater than b, the calf portion of my leg is longer than the thigh portion. If b is greater than c, the calf portion of my leg is shorter than the thigh portion.

3. Waist   a. _____
     Elbow   b. _____
     Subtract b from a   c. _____
		Elbow would hit at waistline. (Line 3a would equal line 3b.)	If c is negative, my arm is short and/or my waist is long. If c is positive, my arm is long and/or my waist is short.

4. Middle-
     fingertip   a. _____
     Mid-thigh   b. _____
		Fingertip would hit mid-thigh. (Line 4a would equal line 4b.)	If b is greater than a, my arm is long and/or my thighs are short. If a is greater than b, my arm is short and/or my thighs are long.

5. Armpit   a. _____
     Waist   b. _____
     Subtract b from a   c. _____
     Waist   d. _____
     Wrist   e. _____
     Subtract e from d   f. _____
		Waist would be located midway between armpit and wrist. (Line 5c would equal line 5f.)	If c is greater than f, I am short waisted and/or long armed. If f is greater than c, I am long waisted and/or short armed.

continued

Body proportion chart *(continued)*

My Measurements		Ideal Measurements	Conclusions
6. Shoulder width	a. _____	Shoulder width would equal neck to waist measurement. (Line 6a would equal line 6b.)	If a is greater than b, I am broad shouldered and/or short waisted. If b is greater than a, I am narrow shouldered and/or long waisted.
Neck to waist	b. _____		
7. Armpit	a. _____	Distance from waist to armpit would equal distance from waist to bottom of derriere. (Line 7c would equal line 7d.)	If c is greater than d, my upper torso is longer than my lower torso or my derrière is small. If d is greater than c, my lower torso is larger than my upper torso or my derrière is large.
Waist	b. _____		
Subtract b from a	c. _____		
Waist to derriere	d. _____		
8. Top of head	a. _____	A person is 7.5 heads tall. (Line 8c multiplied by 7.5 would equal 8a.)	If a is greater than d, my head is small. If a is smaller than d, my head is large.
Chin	b. _____		
Subtract b from a	c. _____		
Multiply c $\times$ 7.5	d. _____		
9. Armpit	a. _____	Nipple no more than 3 inches lower than armpit. (Line 9c would be 3 inches or less.)	If c is greater than 3 inches, my breasts are low. If c is less than 3 inches, my breasts are high.
Nipple	b. _____		
Subtract a from b	c. _____		
10. Shoulder circumference	a. _____	Distance around shoulders would be one inch larger than distance around hips. (Line 10a would be one inch larger than line 10b.)	If a is more than one inch larger than b, my shoulders are broad and/or my hips are small. If b is the same or larger than a, my hips are large and/or my shoulders are narrow.
Hip circumference	b. _____		

continued

Body proportion chart *(continued)*

My Measurements		Ideal Measurements	Conclusions
11. Wrist circumference a. _____		If this measurement is less than 6 inches, you are probably small-boned; if it is more than 6 inches, you are probably large-boned.	I am _____-boned.
12. Bust circumference a. _____ Hip circumference b. _____		Distance around hips would be equal to distance around bust. (Line 12a would equal line 12b.)	If a is greater than b, I am large busted and/or small hipped. If b is greater than a, I am small busted and/or large hipped.
13. Bust circumference a. _____ Waist circumference b. _____ Subtract b from a c. _____		Distance around waist would be 10 inches smaller than distance around bust. (Line 13c would be 10 inches.)	If c is greater than 10 inches, I am large busted and/or small waisted. If c is less than 10 inches, I am small busted and/or large waisted.
14. Hip circumference a. _____ Waist circumference b. _____ Subtract b from a c. _____		Distance around waist would be 10 inches smaller than distance around hips. (Line 14c would be 10 inches.)	If c is less than 10 inches, I am small hipped and/or large waisted. If c is greater than 10 inches, I am large hipped and/or small waisted.
15. Inner corner of left eye to inner corner of right eye a. _____ Inner corner to outer corner of eye b. _____		Distance across eye would equal distance between eyes. (Line 15a would equal line 15b.)	If a is greater than b, my eyes are small and/or wide set. If b is greater than a, my eyes are large and/or close-set.

♀ Analysis of your measurements

Using the Body Proportion Chart, list your possible conclusions (e.g., I am either short waisted or long legged, short waisted or long armed, and so on). Then, take into account how often a characteristic is mentioned and what you already know about your body, writing down your actual conclusions about your body proportions (e.g., I am short waisted, large hipped, small busted).

● ●

Analysis of measurements

Possible conclusions

_____

_____

_____

_____

_____

_____

Actual conclusions

_____

_____

_____

_____

Did you realize that only 10 percent of the population has the ideal proportions as listed on the Body Proportion Chart?—and most ready-made clothing is made according to those proportions. No wonder nearly 50 percent of us require major alterations when we buy ready-to-wear clothing!

Although not as accurate, a simpler way to get a picture of your body proportion and assets is to take a long, squint-eyed look at your two body silhouettes: your profile and face-on views.

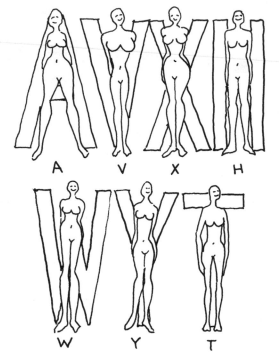

A   V   X   H

W   Y   T

Front view types.

♀ body silhouettes

Using a large magic marker, color in both the profile and face-on body outlines. Step a few feet back and squint at your silhouettes from the front and from the side. Where are you out of balance? Are your hips large and your shoulders small? Are your stomach and hips larger than your bust?

♀ bonnie august system[1]

ANALYSIS OF YOUR BODY

1. Women are shaped primarily as an "A," "V," "X," or "H." Looking at your front view, decide which letter your body most resembles?
2. Women are a "W" if short waisted and a "Y" if long waisted. Women can also be a "T" if thin legs are combined with a heavy torso. The above are all front view letter descriptions. Determine if you are a "W," "Y" or "T"?
3. Looking at your side view, determine if you are a "b," "d," "i," or "r." In each case, think of which letter you resemble.
4. You can be a "b" and "d" (both stomach and derrière are large) but not an "i" and "r" (you can never be both small and large busted). List your body's total descriptive initials:

_____

♀ balance: a key concept

- ▶ If you are an "A," you want to add to your shoulders and upper torso.
- ▶ If you are an "H," you want to minimize your waist.
- ▶ If you are a "Y," you can play down your shoulders.
- ▶ If you are an "X," you may want to deemphasize the shoulders and hips as they are large in comparison to your waist.
- ▶ If you are a "W" add length to your waist.
- ▶ If you are a "Y" shorten your waist.
- ▶ If you are a "T" play down the dichotomy between hip and leg size.
- ▶ If you are an "ibd" add fullness on top to *balance* your bottom.
- ▶ If you are an "r" aim for fullness on the bottom to balance your top.

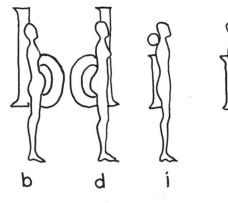

b   d   i   r

Side view types.

♂ body measurements

Go to Chapter 2 questions 46 and 47. Did you list any body challenges in the questionnaire? Even though research shows that men are not as hung up on their body image as women are, it does not hurt to maximize your assets. What did you list as your body assets? The trick is to maximize them by how you dress, while minimizing or deemphasizing your perceived faults. We've spared you the painstakingly analytical section that was an option for the women, but you will need a tape measure and a full-length mirror to take your body measurements and compare them with the ideal model.

● ●

Body assets

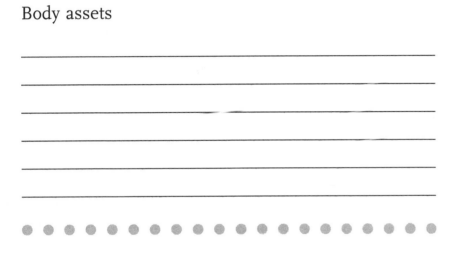

● ●

Take your body measurements and compare them with the ideal model. The drawing shows where to measure and lists classic proportions so you can complete the "Body Proportion Chart."

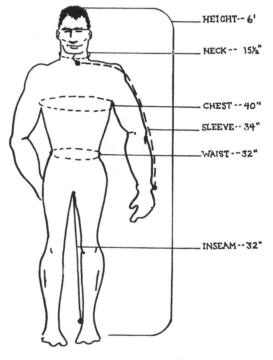

"Ideal" measurements for men.

Body proportion chart

Measurement Directions	My Measurements	Ideal Measurements	Variation
1. Height: Measure without shoes against a wall	_____	6ft	_____
2. Chest: Measure around the fullest part	_____	40 in.	_____
3. Neck size: Measure around the neck at the Adam's apple. For correct shirt neck size add $^1/_2$ inch.	_____	15 $^1/_2$ in.	_____
4. Sleeve measurement: Measure from the prominent bone at the back of the neck along the shoulders over a bent elbow and down to the wrist bone.	_____	34 in.	_____
5. Waist measurement: Measure the natural waistline.	_____	32 in.	_____
6. Trouser inseam: Measure the inside of the crotch point (where the seams meet) to hem.	_____	32 in.	_____

mirror examination

Study your body in a full-length mirror. You will need just that, a full-length mirror, and also a handheld mirror and an old tube of lipstick or a bar of soap. Examine yourself and answer the following questions. To the left of the questions on the "Full-Length Mirror Examination," note what you intend to do about each body part with which you are dissatisfied. Be realistic. Don't say you will wear a girdle if your derrière is protruding if you *must* be comfortable in your clothes.

● ● ● ● ● ● ● ● ● ● ● ● ● ● ● ● ● ●

Full-length mirror examination

1. Head position and size

   a. Do you hold your head straight? _____

   b. Does your head tend to lean toward the side? _____

   c. Is your head large, small, or average? _____

   d. Other observations _____

2. Neck

   a. Is your neck long, short, or average? _____

   b. Is it thick, thin, or average? _____

   c. Other observations _____

3. Chin

   a. Do you have a double or triple chin? _____

   b. Is the base of your chin firm or soft? ___ _____

   c. Is your chin sharp or receding? _____

   d. Other observations _____

4. Eyes

   a. Are your eyes large, small, or average? _____

   b. Are they of equal or unequal size? _____

   c. Are they deep set, protruding, or average? _____

   d. Other observations _____

5. Other Facial Features

   a. Is your forehead low or high? _____

   b. Is your nose long or short? _____

   c. Are your cheeks plump or thin? _____

   d. Is your jaw square or heavy? _____

   e. Other observations _____

6. Ears

   a. Are your ears flat or do they fan out? _____

   b. Are they small, large, or average? _____

   c. Other observations _____

7. Hairline (pull hair away from face and neck)

   a. Does your hairline go down your neck? _____

   b. Draw your hairline from the front:

   c. Draw your hairline from the back:

   d. Other observations _____

8. Hands

   a. Are your fingers long, short, or average? _____

   b. Is your hand small, medium, or large? _____

   c. Other observations _____

9. Shoulders

   a. Are your shoulders sloping, square, wide, narrow, or

      average? _____

   b. Is one shoulder higher than the other? _____

   c. Other observations _____

10. Posture

    a. Do you stand very erect, slump slightly, or slump a lot?

       _____

    b. Do you have an extreme back-hollow? _____

    c. Other observations _____

11. Breasts: Women

    a. Are your breasts equal in size? _____

    b. Is one higher than the other? _____

    c. Are they sagging or firm? _____

    d. Can you support a pencil between your breast and your

       diaphragm? (If you can, you need a bra.)

    e. Is your bust small, medium, large, or extra large? _____

    f. Other observations _____

    Chest: Men

    a. Is your chest muscular or sunken? _____

    b. Is it muscular or soft? _____

    c. Are your breasts prominent? _____

12. Upper Arms

    a. Are your upper arms heavy, thin, or average? _____

    b. Are your upper arms firm or soft? _____

    c. Other observations _____

13. Waist

    a. Is your waist small, medium, or large? _____

    b. Is your waist high or low? _____

    c. Other observations _____

14. Stomach

    a. Is your stomach flat, rounded, or protruding? _____

    b. Is your waist hidden because of your stomach size? _____

    c. Other observations _____

15. Derrière

    a. Is your derrière flat, rounded, protruding, or full? _____

    b. Other observations _____

16. Hips

    a. Is one hip higher than the other? _____

    b. Are your hips narrow, wide, or medium? _____

    c. Other observations _____

17. Thighs

    a. Are your thighs slender, average, or full? _____

    b. Are they smooth or dimpled? _____

    c. Are they firm or flabby? _____

    d. Other observations _____

18. Calves

    a. Are your calves slender, average, or full? _____

    b. Other observations _____

19. Ankles

    a. Are your ankles thick, thin, or average? _____

    b. Other observations _____

20. Feet

    a. Are your feet narrow, average, or wide? _____

    b. Are your feet long, short, or average? _____

    c. Other observations _____

21. Face shape: Place your face with your nose against the mirror and outline your face on the mirror with lipstick or bar soap.

    a. Is your face oval, square, long (oblong), triangular (heart), round, other? _____

    b. Are your cheek bones prominent, high, minimal, other?

    _____

● ●

Women should review Chapter 1, questions 17 to 37, and men should review Chapter 2, questions 25 to 45. After all of this careful body measuring and scrutinizing, what have you learned about your body? How do your body characteristics differ from those you consider to be ideal? Complete the "Differing Body Characteristics" chart. Then, compare your initial observations in Chapter 1 (women) and Chapter 2 (men) with what your tape measure and mirror just told you. Determine if they differed by completing the "Comparison of Observations" chart.

● ●

Differing body characteristics

                              Mine   *Ideal*

_____

_____

_____

_____

_____

● ●

Comparison of observations

Initial observation	*After measurements*
_____	_____
_____	_____
_____	_____

● ●

Now look at your characteristics listed in the chart, "Differing Body Characteristics." Are you unsatisfied with those parts of yourself, or are you merely observing the variation? Place a star (*) beside all those body characteristics that you want to camouflage or hide. These are your body challenges. Do they match the items you listed in the questionnaire? All the remaining characteristics are assets. Determine if your assets outnumber your faults. List your primary assets. Then, ask five persons to tell you what they like best about your body.

Place a star beside those body characteristics you want to camouflage or hide.

● ●

Primary assets

Your opinion

_____

_____

_____

Opinions of others

1. _____

2. _____

3. _____

4. _____

5. _____

● ●

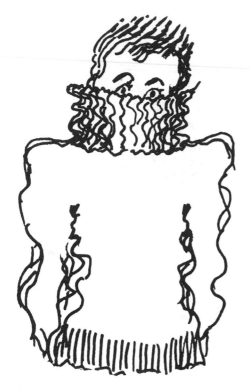

I know I can't wear high turtlenecks, so I
must have a short neck.

Would you prefer to lengthen the look of
your neck or shorten the look of your face?

Although it is interesting to know what others think, only you can really decide what body parts you want to highlight. You have lived with that body for a lot of years and know it pretty well. Remember to be nice to yourself. Change your emphasis from the faults to the assets.

Look at the "to emphasize" column of the following "Clothing Tricks" chart. What do those clothing items say about your body. For example, "I know I can't wear high turtlenecks, therefore I must have a short neck?"

Now look at your list of the starred "Differing Body Characteristics" chart. Place a check (✓) beside all characteristics you want to deemphasize on the following "Clothing Tricks" charts, and study the types of clothing you should wear when you want to play these features down. Place a star (*) beside the features you want to emphasize on the "Clothing Tricks" charts and study the types of clothing you should wear when you want to play up these features.

If the emphasize column lists one clothing item that is also in the deemphasize column under another of your body characteristics, then you can decide which is the more important characteristic to accentuate or camouflage. For example, if you have a long face and a short neck, then decide if you would rather lengthen the look of your neck or shorten your face. If your face is way too long and your neck a little short, you wouldn't want to wear the low V-neckline. But if you have an extremely short neck and a relatively long face, you would want to wear the low V-neckline. Check out the chart on the page 142 for a shortcut.

The right hairstyle can also go a long way to emphasize the positive. The "Emphasize the Positive" chart will show you a few of these tricks.

Don't worry about the categories on the following charts that don't pertain to your body. And remember it is balance, line, and emphasis that help you accentuate your assets. Sometimes it is as simple as raising your hands to loosen your shirt that will lengthen the look of a too-short waist. Usually we are long-legged in combination with short-waisted, and balance is the key. Stitching, tucks, stripes, or a banded-front will carry the eye vertically, lengthening the look of the torso. And don't forget our friend, color: use the same tone belt as your shirt and the eye will add the belt width onto your torso length, thereby balancing your upper and lower body.

Clothing tricks for the face

FEATURE	TO DEEMPHASIZE	TO EMPHASIZE

A round face	V-necklines
	Pointed collars
	Off-center pins or
	  scarves
	Boutonniere or
	  hanky
	Necktie
		Round necklines
		High necklines
		Turtle necklines
		Repeating the line of
		  the face
		Round glasses
		Bow tie

A square face	Round or V-necklines	Square necklines Square glasses
A heart-shaped face	Square or oval necklines	Wide V-necklines Heart lockets Lolita glasses Club tie with hearts
A long face	Turtlenecks Round and cowl collars Scarves	Low V-necklines

An oval face	Any line other than
	  oval
		Oval lines repeating
		  face shape

Clothing tricks for the neck

FEATURE	TO DEEMPHASIZE	TO EMPHASIZE

A narrow neck	Turtle neck
	Ascot ties
	Stand-up collars
	Ruffles and soft scarf
	  arrangements
	Exact fitting, buttoned-
	  up collar
		Low or skimpy lines
		Exposure of bony areas
		Buttoned-up collar,
		  too loose

A large or wide
  neck
	Narrow long collar
	V-necklines
	Pointed collars
	Plain necklines
	Exact fitting, buttoned-
	  up collar
		Wide or spread collar
		High, turtleneck
		Crew neck
		Wide ruffles
		Buttoned-up collar,
		  too tight

Clothing tricks for the neck

FEATURE	TO DEEMPHASIZE	TO EMPHASIZE
A short neck	Unbuttoned shirt Low V- or U-necklines Jewelry on chains Long pointed collar Hats with a high crown	Buttoned-up shirt High, turtleneck Ruffles Spread collar

A long neck	Closed collar
	Ascot ties
	Turtle and stand-up
	  collars
	Mandarin collars
	Scarves
		Open collar
		Low V- or
		  U-necklines

Clothing tricks for the shoulders

FEATURE	TO DEEMPHASIZE	TO EMPHASIZE

Square or broad shoulders	Trim, narrow sleeves
	Lines that draw the eye
	  away from shoulder
	Deep and narrow
	  necklines
	Downward pointing lapels
	Open jacket
	Kimono or raglan sleeves
	Side-front and back
	  vertical seams
	Medium-width collars
	  and lapels
	Lapel pin
	Slanted front yoke
		Boat necklines
		Epaulets
		Shoulder padding
		Trim around the
		  shoulders
		Wide neckline and collars
		Buttoned up jacket
		Sleeveless clothes
		  extending down arm
		Wide horizontal designs
		Horizontal yokes
		Cap, dolman or puffy
		  sleeves

Sloping or narrow shoulders	Wide V
	Shallow and square
	  necklines
	Small collars
	Set-in sleeves with
	  fullness
	Cap sleeves
	Padded shoulders
	Wider, upward-pointing
	  lapels
	Front and back yokes
	Epaulets
	Puffed sleeves
		Raglan and dolman
		  sleeves
		Sleeveless and halter tops
		Tank tops
		Muscle shirts
		Small straps and strapless
		  dresses

Clothing tricks for the chest

FEATURE	TO DEEMPHASIZE	TO EMPHASIZE
A large bust or chest	Plain, loose-fitting bodices Vertical lines and tucks and stripes Single-breasted styles Wrapped blouses, dresses, jackets High yokes Narrow capes Straight-lined or slightly flared coat	Low yokes Double-breasted styles Details at bustline Breast pockets Close-fitting clothes Empire or high-waisted lines Short sleeves or necklaces ending at bustline
A small bust or chest	Breast pockets Full sleeves and details that create the look of fullness High waistlines and empire styles Low front yoke with gathers Blousy styles Horizontal stripes Ruffles	Tight sweaters Narrow lines Low necklines
A low bust	An uplift bra Plain bodices that do not show the outline of the figure	Low cut necklines Tight sweaters Empire waists

Clothing tricks for the arms

FEATURE	TO DEEMPHASIZE	TO EMPHASIZE
Long arms	Full sleeves Cuffs Mid-arm sleeves and trims Contrasting sleeves	Skimpy sleeves Sleeveless styles Styles with very short sleeves
Short arms	Sleeveless styles Long, fitted sleeves	Large cuffs Puffy and mid-arm styles

Clothing tricks for the arms

FEATURE	TO DEEMPHASIZE	TO EMPHASIZE
Full arms	Loose sleeves Slim sleeves if not too tight Short sleeves ending two inches above elbow and not binding arm Sleeves ending at narrowest part of arm	Tight cuffs Tightly fitted and trimmed sleeves Sheer fabrics Sleeveless clothes Muscle shirts Cap sleeves Sleeves ending at widest part of arm
Thin arms	Short sleeves ending two inches above elbow and not binding arm Slim sleeves if not too tight Full, long sleeves Trims and cuffs	Very tight, thin or sleeveless styles Sheer fabrics Cap sleeves

Clothing tricks for the abdomen

FEATURE	TO DEEMPHASIZE	TO EMPHASIZE
Large abdomen	Longer jackets, sweaters and vests Supporting girdle Overblouses or shirts Details above waist Self-fabric belts Small over-all print fabric Slanted front or side-seam pockets Suspenders/braces Pant waist at waistline Ease in waistline (go up a size?) Back or side zipper Beltless dresses A-lines Gathered skirts	Tight belts Clinging fabrics Patch pockets Front zipper Pants riding below belly

Clothing tricks for the legs

FEATURE	TO DEEMPHASIZE	TO EMPHASIZE
Long legs	Horizontal lines Hem interest Pants with cuffs Tunics Longer jackets—end right below crotch Tiered and full skirts	High-waisted styles Pleats Vertical lines Pants with no cuffs No horizontal lines Shorts Extremely short skirts
Short legs	Higher heels Shorter jackets High-waisted styles Cuffless pants A and princess lines Longer hemlines	Horizontal lines Short skirts on full legs Cuffed pants Longer jacket
Slender or full legs	Medium full skirts Pleats Skirts long enough to hit best part of leg Detail interest on upper body Neutral socks or hose that match shoes	Tight pants Pencil-slim skirts Too short skirts Dark or colored socks or hose that contrast with shoe Bermuda or walking shorts

Clothing tricks for the torso

FEATURE	TO DEEMPHASIZE	TO EMPHASIZE
Heavy thighs or wide hips	Details above the waist that help to balance width Pants with slight flare or straight leg Front pant tucks Jackets end at crotch Loose sweaters and vests A-line, gored, slightly full, dirndl skirts and dresses	Pants tapering at ankle Closely fitting pants Clinging materials Full pleats Gathers Hip interest (pockets) Tightly tucked-in shirts

Clothing tricks for the torso

FEATURE	TO DEEMPHASIZE	TO EMPHASIZE
Flat or protruding derrière	Jackets, cardigan sweaters ending anywhere but the butt Skirts not drooping longer or shorter in back Dirndl gored, A-line skirts Pleated, tiered, flared skirts Soft waistline gathers around slim skirt Loose-fitting trouser	Skimpy lines Clinging fabrics Tight, fitted skirts or trousers Uneven hem lengths Sweater/jacket ending at largest part of protruding derrière
A large or wide waist	Ease of fit Matching belt Lines that carry the eye toward the vertical center of the figure Vest, jacket, sweater worn unbuttoned Slim, straight dresses, jumpers, overblouses, gently tapered at waistline Princess lines	Contrasting belt Bright or wide sashes and belts Tightly fitted clothing at waistline
A small or narrow waist	Untucked shirt Interesting buckles, chains and belts Loose-fitting clothing Straight-lined dresses and coats	Cinching in tightly Fitted shirt, tightly tucked in Closely fitted waistline
A high waist	Dropped waistlines Belts matching top Vertical seams and tucks on blouses and dresses Skirts and pants without waistbands Untucked shirt	Raised waistlines Contrasting belts Belts matching bottom

Clothing tricks for the torso

FEATURE	TO DEEMPHASIZE	TO EMPHASIZE
A low waist	Raised waistlines Attention above the waist Belts matching bottom A-line dresses	Low belts Trims that call attention to the waist Belts matching top

You would reverse the colored belt to shorten a too-long waist: match the belt tone to the skirt or slacks. Then you wouldn't use vertical lines on the shirt because you wouldn't want your waist to look any longer than it already is.

Keep focusing on balance, line, and emphasis, and you can successfully camouflage your body faults. Following are more examples to drive home the importance of these concepts:

balance

Balance heavy thighs and small chests with fullness in the torso; broad shoulders and thin hips with ease in the pant. Bulky and shiny fabrics will make you look heavier, so wear these textures where you want to add quantity. Smooth, lightweight, matte-finish materials are streamlining, so wear these where you want to minimize quantity. Lightweight, clingy, shiny fabrics, however, reveal rather than camouflage what they cover.

line

If you want to deemphasize a square jaw, don't wear a square neckline or square glasses. To repeat a body line with clothing only calls attention to the body part you are trying to camouflage. Diagonal lines are wonderful for the body. They keep the eye moving so that faults seem to slide away rather than become the focus of attention. Diagonals camouflage both excessive height and width, and can be worn successfully by most people. The V-neckline is the most versatile and flattering of necklines. Curved lines emphasize roundness. Straight lines emphasize angularity.

Straight lines emphasize angularity.

Create the illusion of ideal measurements

IF YOU ARE:	SHORT	TALL	HEAVY	THIN
Line	Accentuate up and down lines. Jacket must be correct length: barely cover derrière. Shorter jackets make legs appear longer and person appear taller. Think vertical.	Contrasts in color of jacket and trousers. No narrow, prominent, vertical stripes. Think horizontal.	Subtle vertical stripes, one-color schemes, loose fit. Sleeves tapered. Fitted jacket. Think vertical.	Details that increase body width: pleats and cuffed trousers: peaked/wide lapels. Think horizontal.
Color	One overall color or darkness. No contrasts between jacket and skirt/slacks.	Color contrasts. Dark top decreases apparent size.	Dull, dark, cool colors. No pale or bright colors.	Bright, light warm colors.
Texture	Smooth types: sharkskin, gabardine, smooth worsteds, soft tweeds and knits.	Textured fabrics: cheviot wool, twists, tweeds, shetlands and flannels.	Smooth fabrics. No heavy or light weight fabrics that crease easily. Neatness very important.	Bulky fabrics: wide-wale corduroy, tweeds, cheviot wool, flannel.
Style	Single-breasted, two or three button style. A long lapel line. No wide lapels. Slightly built shoulders.	Two- or three-button suits with wide spacing. Moderate rolled lapels. Jacket accenting width: double-breasted or Edwardian. Shoulders squared. Waist fit loose. Pocket flaps.	No wide lapels. Long roll lapels. Shirts with plackets (front panel containing button holes).	Double-breasted with wide lapels. No sack-like styles, but an easy fit is better than tight. Vests add bulk.
Pattern	Narrow stripes and herringbones. Miniature, muted plaids.	Subtle plaids. Checks, herringbones widely spaced and in soft tones.	Muted tweeds, faint plaids, large scale vertical stripes. No more than two patterns as too much contrast breaks up vertical line.	No obvious vertical stripes. Patterns that add width, such as plaids.

Characteristic   YES   NO

Low Forehead

High Forehead

Large Nose

Small Nose

Short Neck

Long Neck

Wide Jaw

Narrow Jaw

Protruding Chin

Receding Chin

Emphasize the positive.

If you're always saying dumb things, you might want to try black scarves and red shoes.

emphasis

Our faces are primary assets for most of us. Brilliant thoughts come from those mouths of ours. So a bright-colored scarf, tie, or braces will emphasize your head and the words you say. Color carries the eye, so use it to carry the eye where you want it to go. Bright or light colors attract attention. Light, bright, clear, warm colors tend to make you look heavier, so don't wear red on your hips if you don't want to emphasize your hips. Cool, dark, muted colors are more discreet. They tend to minimize size.

If you want to emphasize your height, keep the same color family (e.g., burgundy, deep rose, medium rose) or value (darkness and lightness) going from shoe to neck. If we wear black shoes, navy socks or hose, navy pants or skirt, and charcoal blazer the eye moves vertically, increasing our height in the process. Wear a vertically striped shirt or a pin striped suit to further heighten the look.

In contrast, if you want to deemphasize your height, wear horizontals to stop the eyes' movement upward (e.g., wear khaki trousers with that navy blazer). The eye now starts at the shoes, is immediately interrupted by the horizontal shoe top and pant bottom, and stops again at the jacket hem. After three color changes the eye has stopped two times. Your height has been diminished in the process.

If your hips are larger than you would like, you never want a jacket or sweater to stop at the largest part of your hips. Again, the line of the hem will draw others' eyes right where you want them not to go. And if you emphasize this hem line by contrasting the color of jacket or sweater and skirt or slacks (e.g., white blazer with navy pants) the eye will be pulled all the more forcefully right to the largest part of your hips.

proportion

Very closely related to balance is proportion. Proportion is a subtle, elusive word that is defined as the relationship of one quantity to another. As one varies, so does the other. The result of correct proportion is balance, harmony, and symmetry. One key design premise ties in closely to appealing proportion. That premise is: uneven quantities are more appealing to the eye than even quantities. Think about decorating a table in your house. If you place one item on it, say a candle, it looks good. If you put a second item, another candle perhaps, it looks wrong. Just add a third item and again the arrangement is appealing to the eye. One, three, five look better than two, four, or six. How does this principal apply to dressing, you ask? If the only jewelry near your face is obvious gold earrings and a gold chain the look will be good (provided it is quality jewelry and goes with the mood and style of the blouse/sweater or jacket). It is because three gold pieces are seen as a group. Three is an uneven number and uneven quantities are appealing to the eye. Add another chain and your look will be off. Now you're wearing four. Less is more in this case. Or more can be better—add another chain and get a total of five gold pieces. This will look good.

The same principal applies more strongly to quantities of clothing mass. Don't divide your body in half with a jacket, rather let it be off—either larger or smaller than half. Similarly, your suit jacket should not equally divide your jacket-skirt or jacket-pant unit. This is more obvious when you are wearing a jacket and bottom of differing colors. The unappealingness of halves also applies to quarters, although the chances are less for you to divide your body clothing unit into four equal parts.

Did you know that a large head makes you look shorter and a small head makes you look taller? Although you can't shave off head size, you can wear hair that is short and styled close to your head. So if you concluded that you have a head that is large in proportion to the rest of your body, wear your hair to minimize its size. Your hair works well when it is in proportion to your face. People with delicate faces and small features can wear close-cropped hairdos more easily than their large-faced friends. Eyeglasses are attractive when they are correctly proportioned to your body and head size—not too tiny if you're large, not too large if you're small, keeping in mind the current styles.

Consider scale. A large print fabric on a small frame may be overwhelming, a too-small print on a large frame may look absurd. A tiny woman carrying a tiny purse works; a big woman carrying a tiny purse doesn't work. A small man in a large distinct plaid is not in scale.

Your best tool for balance and proportion is your full-length mirror.

Don't divide your body exactly in half with a jacket. Let it be greater than or less than half.

fit

You can balance your body's imbalance, wear lines, colors, textures, and details that draw the eye to your primary assets, and the look will still not be right if the fit is off. Be certain of fit!

Let's go through some areas that are real bugaboos for fit.

Consider scale. A large print on a small frame may be overwhelming. A too-small print on a large frame may look absurd.

front zippers

Most women develop "little tummies" as they grow older and these protrusions often cause zippers to protrude right along with the tummy. The best place for zippers for women is in the back and second best on the side, but many ready-made women's items come with front zippers. Just be certain there is no pulling or straining on the zipper placket. Men are stuck with front zippers. So beware! Be sure your waistband is large enough.

slacks

Slacks present many fitting problems. Acquaint yourself with the look of well-cut, properly fitting pants. They should look and feel comfortable at the waist, flow smoothly over hips, hang straight from the hipline, not bind at the crotch or "smile" under the derrière, and should cover the top of the shoe in back. Ankles should not show when you are standing. Fashion may allow for varying lengths, but above are the guidelines for the classic slack fit. And be conscious of the location of your waist. For the classic fit, you will want waist-lines of slacks and skirts to ride comfortably at that waistline. If you are not sure you know where your waist really is, tie a string tautly in the waist area and see where it goes automatically. Your waist is not always at your navel. Even if your waist is large, you will look neat and well dressed if your skirt or slack fits easily at your waist.

Always buy large enough clothing. It may be hard to admit you need a bigger size, but too-small clothing tells everyone else you should have gone up a size. It suggests you've gained weight. You are only trying to fool yourself if you squeeze into a small size that you wish might work. And the look is cheap!

shirts

Shirt collars can cause a problem for men who wear ties. Be certain to have your neck size measured carefully (neck circumference plus one half-inch.) If you have an unusually wide or narrow neck, you may need to have your shirts tailor-made, or to purchase them from a high-end store with ordering resources.

Whether we expand or our shirts shrink, many women end up with gapping at the bust line—even with small busts! You can sew down a blouse that you are sure has shrunk. If you do this, be careful to leave enough room for your head to fit through the top and to *match* the thread and stitching perfectly! Or if you are making a shirt, place a button directly between your breasts and adjust the remaining button positioning from there.

blazer jacket

Although you may not wear your jacket buttoned, it should button smoothly. Sure enough you will be fidgeting with the buttons one day when you are nervous. It will make you all the more nervous if your jacket pulls awkwardly or, worse yet, doesn't even pull together at all. You are announcing, "My jacket is too small."

If your jacket has a back vent, it should hang perpendicular to the floor. For the classic fit, jacket sleeves would end at your wrist bones, with your shirt cuff extending one-fourth to one-half inch beyond the jacket sleeve. The jacket should lie smoothly across the shoulders with no bubble behind the neck. Using a curved hanger will facilitate this fit. Your shirt collar should extend above the jacket collar one-fourth to one-half inch.

Fit is important, especially when there is a body discrepancy, such as a large waist with small shoulders. Don't think there is something wrong with you when clothes don't fit. No two people are alike. Have your clothes altered when they need it, or learn to do it yourself. Don't regard alterations as too much trouble. They are not. Take the time to determine your problems with fit and how you plan to address them.

●●●●●●●●●●●●●●●●●●●●●●

Fit

Problems

_____

_____

_____

_____

_____

_____

Corrective actions

_____

_____

_____

_____

_____

_____

_____

_____

●●●●●●●●●●●●●●●●●●●●●●

♀ women

● ●

Circumference measurements

List the following circumference measurements from the chart on page 120:

bust _____

waist _____

hips _____

thigh _____

calf _____

ankle _____

neck _____

● ●

The experts say you may be "too large" if your tape measure shows any of the following. List the measurements requested in your journal and determine if you are "too large" in any of the above areas.

▸ Your bust is more than 10 inches larger than your waist.
▸ Your hips are more than 3 inches larger than your bust.
▸ Your thigh is more than 8 inches larger than your calf.
▸ Your calf is more than 6 inches larger than your ankle.
▸ Your neck is the same as, or larger than, your calf.

● ●

Areas in which you are "too large"

_____

_____

_____

_____

_____

● ●

Perhaps it is okay with you to be large? Perhaps the rest of you is just "too small."

♂ men

Look at your measurements on page 128, and complete the journal entries.

● ●

Your "too-large" areas

_____

_____

_____

_____

_____

● ●

Your "too-small" areas

_____

_____

_____

● ●

Is it okay with you to be too large or too small?

men and women

Some people are constantly battling weight and doing all kinds of things to make themselves feel guilty when they gain weight. The best philosophy is simply: *Accept yourself at the weight you are now*

Horizontal wrinkles indicate clothing is too tight. Vertical wrinkles indicate clothing is too loose.

or do something about changing that weight. If the desired change is weight loss, then you can only lose weight by aerobically exercising *and* cutting calories. One will not work without the other.

But big can be brilliant! And if you decide to enjoy your size, then get all of those too-small clothes out of your closet. You don't have to get rid of them yet if you're not quite convinced that you will not be able to wear them again. You can store them. But do not keep them in eyesight.

Busy, effective people wear clothes they can move around in comfortably. Keep in mind that looser clothes are better than tighter clothes. A good rule of thumb is that your clothing have a one inch give from wherever you pull them.

Horizontal wrinkles usually indicate something is too tight. Vertical wrinkles indicate your clothing is too loose. If your clothing is too loose, you can look dowdy or sloppy.

Correct posture can help your fit tremendously. If you stand with your body aligned from head to toe your clothing will fall properly. Your backbone straight, your chin back, tailbone pulled down, shoulders back: in yoga we call it *tadasana* (mountain). In dancing we say head over shoulders, shoulders over hips, hips over feet. And in other visual terms we can think of correct posture being the way we would stand if a helium balloon was attached to the center of our head, or if puppet strings were pulling us upward from our head and shoulders.

Think about tucking your tailbone down. The tailbone-down position also helps your stomach bulge. In fact, it is healthier to flatten your stomach by the tailbone-down movement than the stomach-tight movement. Stand up now and try tilting your tailbone up and then pulling it down. Get the feel of the down position.

Now try each of the correct posture visualizations mentioned above: helium balloon, puppet, *tadasana* (mountain), and dancer alignment. Determine which works best for you.

Practice correct posture! It is a habit that can be developed, and the first step is awareness.

review

What do you remember about this chapter that is significant to *you?* First, list surprises, "ahas," lightbulbs in the page of your journal that follows. Then, look back through this chapter and list those discoveries you want to highlight.

● ●

Review: chapter 5

"Ahas"

1. _____

_____

2. _____

_____

3. _____

_____

Discoveries to highlight

_____

_____

_____

_____

_____

_____

_____

The review page at the end of this chapter will be useful later as you want to review *Dress Smart*. You won't need to reread the chapter, just your "ahas."

endnote

1. Bonnie August, *Looking Thin: The Famous Designer's Guide to Reshaping Your Body and Concealing Almost Any Figure Flaw with Clothes,* New York: Rawson Associates, 1981.

employ color

6

color facts

Did you realize that some colors make you look older and others make you look younger? Some colors accentuate circles and blemishes and others minimize them? With some colors next to your face you seem more bright and alive. Your face will appear smooth and flawless. Other colors seem to cry out for more and more make-up . . . or sleep! Some colors you wear will make your face, green or gray, while others, even though very nearly the same, are different enough to add rosiness and radiance. Are your colors working for you?

Let's begin looking at color by defining the language. Read quickly through the following color vocabulary and use it along with the color wheel on the next page, as a reference while we analyze "Employ Color" questions in Chapters 1 and 2.

Now let's review some color facts. *All colors come from five basic pigments:* the three primary colors (red, yellow, blue), and black and white. Theoretically, an artist could mix all the millions of other col-

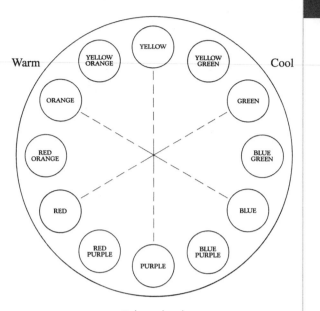

Color wheel

Warm | **Cool**

COLOR VOCABULARY

1. Primary Colors: red, yellow, blue
2. Secondary Colors: green, orange, violet. These are made by mixing two primary colors
3. Tertiary Colors (Intermediate): red-orange, yellow-orange, yellow-green, blue-green, blue-violet, red-violet. Two-word colors that are made by mixing a primary and secondary color
4. Spectrum Colors: representative of each color family in purest and most intense form
5. Value: darkness or lightness of a color (amount of white or toner added)
   tint: mixed with white
   tone: gray by color opposite it on color wheel (complement)
   shade: mixed with black
6. Toners: black, gray, complementary color or a dark color to be mixed with a clear color
7. Clear: —without toners—clean, pure
8. Muted: with the addition of toners—dirty, grayed, murky
9. Warm: red-orange side of color wheel: red, orange, yellow (associated with fire, earth, sun). Yellow- and red-based colors are warm
10. Cool: blue-green side of color wheel: green, blue, blue-violet (associated with sea, sky, foliage) Blue-based colors are cool
11. Chroma: intensity or saturation of a color
12. Hue: another word for color, the quality by which one color is distinguished from another
13. Complements: colors across from each other on the color wheel
14. Expressive or discordant colors: colors not in harmony— exciting, provocative
15. Pigment (colorant): a substance imparting black, white, or color to other materials

ors from these five pigments or dyes. Printers do this to produce the full-color pictures in magazines. They use red, yellow, blue, and black ink with white paper. In reality, it is more complicated; but in theory, it is neat and simple. Your personal coloring is achieved in much the same way. Body pigments called carotene (yellow), oxyhemoglobin (red-blue), and melanin (yellow-brown) make up the color of your skin, hair, and eyes.

Melanin is the protective pigment and is what increases as we tan in the summertime. Do you notice that you appear a bit more golden, tan, or amber in the summer?

Some of us will have more carotene than oxyhemoglobin. As a result, we will appear as peachy-skinned whites, golden-brown blacks, or yellow-undertoned Orientals, Indians, or dark-skinned nationalities.

Others will have a predominance of oxyhemoglobin. If you are such a person, you will appear as a rosy-skinned white, a red-blue or ebony black, or a blue-undertoned Oriental, Indian, or dark-skinned person. All of us, except albinos, will have three pigments in varying amounts. We all have our unique formulas. Let's look at some examples on a scale of one to ten, with the melanin listed first, oxyhemoglobin second, and carotene last in each case. Person A might be 5:8:3, and Person B might be 7:3:9. If both are Caucasian, would A (5:8:3) appear rosier or peachier than B (7:3:9)? Who would tan the most in the summer? Who would be more likely to have red hair?

Now on to the second color fact: the *eye sees comparisons*. No color is seen in isolation but in relation to nearby colors.

Therefore, the eye sees colors near your face in relation to the color of your skin, hair, and eyes. As we grew up, many of us were taught to accentuate the color of our eyes by the color of clothing we wore. For many of us, our eyes are one of our best features and there is good reason to accentuate that asset. There is, however, greater quantity of skin and hair than eyes. So the colors we wear in our blouses, ties, scarves, jackets, jewelry and glasses work best if they go with our skin and our hair. Our eyes are still important and certain colors will certainly do wonderful things for our eyes (make them shine, make the whites whiter, emphasize the sparkle). But if the wrong colors are next to our skin, we see aging, sallowing, muddying; accentuating of lines, blemishes, wrinkles, shadows, or circles. The right colors will do the opposite and make us appear younger, more radiant, and smoother. They clarify our complexion and minimize facial lines, shadows, and circles.

Those colors that match our hair or at least are the same approximate warmth of color look good. For example, rose beige (cool) is better than golden tan (warm) for a person with ash blonde hair (cool).

So, our body pigmentation determines which colors look good near our faces. Our wardrobes start with us. We are the basic colors in our wardrobes, and additional colors must coordinate with us!

We can all wear colors from each color family, but certain ones within each family are better on us. And they are much more obviously better on some of us than on others.

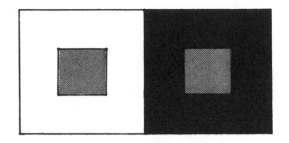

The center square in each of these squares is the same color. Only the surrounding squares differ.

The skin tone is the same for each of these women. Only the colors surrounding their faces are different.

five principles of color selection

How do you determine which colors look best on you? There are five basic principles involved. Let's now take each one and see how it applies.

1. *You can wear either yellow-based colors or blue-based colors better.*

What is meant by that? Blue-based colors are usually cool. They are the colors associated with the sky, forest, and sea. They are on the right side of the color wheel (see page 154). Yellow-based colors are warm colors. They are associated with the sun and fire, and are on the left side of the color wheel. Red is also a warm color, but because primary red contains no yellow, it is not yellow-based. Blue can be warmer if it contains yellow. You can cool down yellow by adding blue. You can take almost any color and make it warmer or cooler by adding yellow or blue. Adding red also warms up colors, but the addition of this primary color does not affect the appearance of our skin as much as adding blue or yellow.

Think of blue-pink and peach. Consider which one is better for you? Peach is a warm pink that is yellow-based. It is a combination of yellow, red, and white. Blue-pink, on the other hand, is a mix of blue, red, and white and is a cooler pink than peach. If you don't know which looks better on you, check it out. Do you have a couple of scarves in these colors? How about clothing or scraps of fabrics? Hold them one at a time under your chin. Look at what the color does to your face.

As you check out each of the five principles be sure to:

wear no makeup
observe in daylight
look at your face, not at the color

What good or bad things is that color doing to your skin, hair, and eyes? If all you see is the color and not the face, the color is too strong for your pigmentation. The color is wearing you; you are not wearing the color.

If you have nothing peach or blue-pink at home, go to a fabric store and hold up bolts or remnants of fabric next to your face. Use the above techniques also to test the following principles.

2. *You can wear either clear or muted colors better.*

Clear colors include pure, jewel tones, crayon colors, fresh, crisp, vivid, and bright colors. Muted colors have had toners added (grays, blacks, ochers, or umbers) to the clear pigments. They appear murky, dirty, or toned. Think of the differences between clear fuchsia (dark blue-pink) and dusty rose, royal blue and denim blue, clear primary yellow and mustard gold. Determine which you wear better?

3. *You can wear either light tints or dark tones better.*

Think of pastel pink and burgundy, pale powder blue or navy blue, light and dark teal blue. Some of us are lucky enough to be able to wear both light and dark values. Think of how striking some people look with chocolate or cream next to their faces.

4. *You can wear high or low contrasts better.*

Some high-contrast combinations are black and white, navy with icy yellow, chocolate brown with creamy ivory. Examples of low-contrast color combinations are navy blue with denim-blue, burgundy with rose, chocolate brown with caramel brown. Consider whether high- or low-contrast combinations work better for you.

5. *You can wear every color that is on your body.*

In your blue or brown eyes, there may be gold or yellow-orange. Those are good yellow-oranges and golds for you. The blues or browns are good also. Point your index finger to the ground and squeeze the blood toward the finger tip. What is the color of red? Is it blue-red or orange-red? That red will be good on you. You may not like beiges and tans right next to your neck and face, but you will like those which are bluer (rose beige) if you have a predominance of blue in your skin and those which are more yellow (caramel beige) if you have a yellow undertone to your skin. Notice how wonderful gray looks on a person with gray hair. Look at the tweedy black/gray sport coat on a black-haired person whose hair is turning gray. If you have ever frosted your hair ivory, you will notice that you can now wear ivory clothing because it matches the frosting. The ivory may still not do the wonderful things for your skin that a soft white does, but it works because it works with your hair.

To determine your best colors, complete the chart, "My Color Season." The numbers in the chart under women and men refer to the question numbers in Chapter 1 (women) and Chapter 2 (men). In the chart, copy the letter of your answers to the questions indicated. If you have no answer marked in the original questionnaire, write NA (not applicable). If the question applies, but you are not certain of the answer, try to use what you have learned to complete it now.

Once you have filled in the chart, circle your answers to each question in the four Section Tables that follow. Each Section Table represents a different "color" personality. Count up the number of matches you have with each Section Table (count the number of cir-

Have you ever frosted your hair and discovered that you can now wear ivory?

cled letters) and write the totals in the chart provided to see with which section you have the greatest number of matches. Then, read the descriptions.

● ● ● ● ● ● ● ● ● ● ● ● ● ● ● ● ● ● ● ●

My color season

Women		*Men*	
A.	41. _____	A.	49. _____
B.	42. _____	B.	50. _____
C.	43. _____	C.	51. _____
D.	44. _____	D.	52. _____
E.	45. _____	E.	53. _____
F.	46. _____	F.	54. _____
G.	47. _____	G.	55. _____
H.	48. _____	H.	56. _____
I.	49. _____	I.	57. _____
J.	50. _____	J.	58. _____
K.	51. _____	K.	59. _____
L.	52. _____	L.	60. _____
M.	53. _____	M.	61. _____
N.	54. _____	N.	62. _____
O.	55. _____	O.	63. _____

Section 1

A. a, b, d, e, f

B. a, b, d, g, h, not applicable (NA)

C. b, d, f, g, h, i, NA

Section 2

A. a, b, d, f

B. a, b, d, g, h, NA

C. b, d, f, h, i, NA

D. a, b, c, e, f, NA

E. b, c, d, e, f, NA

F. NA

G. a, b, c, e, f, h, j

H. b, NA

I. a

J. c, d, e, f

K. b, d, e, f

L. a, c, d, f

M. a

N. b

O. a

D. a, b, e, f, NA

E. NA

F. NA

G. f, h, i, j

H. b, c, NA

I. b

J. b, f

K. d, f

L. a, b, c, d, f, g, i

M. a

N. a

O. b

Section 3

A. a, b, c, d, e, f

B. c, e, f, g, h, NA

C. a, b, c, f, g, i, NA

D. b, d, e, f, NA

E. a, c, d, e, f, NA

F. a, b, c, d, e, f, g, h

G. a, b, c, d, g, i, j

H. a, NA

I. d

J. a, f

K. b, c, f

L. b, g, h, j

M. b

N. b

O. a

Section 4

A. a, b, c, d, e, f

B. c, e, f, g, h, NA

C. a, b, c, f, g, j, NA

D. b, d, e, f, NA

E. a, c, d, e, f, NA

F. a, b, c, d, f, g, h, NA

G. a, b, c, d, e, g, i, j

H. a, c, NA

I. c

J. a, d, f

K. a, f

L. a, b, c, e, g, h, i, j

M. b

N. a

O. b

● ●

Totals

Record the number of matches you have in each section.

Section 1 _____

Section 2 _____

Section 3 _____

Section 4 _____

● ●

color classifications

section 1

Your overall appearance may be regal. Bernice Kratner, *Color Me a Season*, has found connections between certain eye patterns and colors people wear best. Your eye pattern could include a part of the pupil (black center of eye) touching the outside edge of the iris (the colored part around the black pupil), or small lines outside your pupil that resemble the spokes of a wheel, or birthmark-looking spots in your iris. You will wear clear, cool colors, with high contrasts and mixed values well. Carol Jackson's *Color Me Beautiful* would classify you as a "winter," JoAnne Wallace's *Dress With Style* would call you a "cool winter," while Joanna Nicholson and Judy Lewis-Crum's *Color Wonderful* would call you a "contrast."

section 2

Your overall appearance may be colorless. You probably suntan little or fade immediately when you do tan. You have a delicate, transparent look to your skin and are very dependent on makeup and clothing colors. Your eye pattern may look like broken glass or waves. You wear cool, muted colors, pastels (tints), and low contrasts best. You would be called a "summer" or "cool summer" or "gentle" according to the various classification categories.

section 3

Your overall appearance may be metallic. Your iris could look like an Aztec sun or a many-pointed star. Your eyes may contain obvious flecks of gold. You most likely wear muted, warm, low-contrast colors.

You would be classified as an "autumn," "warm autumn," or "muted."

section 4

Your overall appearance may be described as radiant. You blush easily. You could have naturally rosy cheeks and a vibrant, lively skin tone. Your iris might contain rays of sunlight radiating either directly from the pupil or from a space around the pupil. You will best wear vivid, glowing colors that are clear and warm and pure. You will look great in high-contrast colors. You most likely are a "spring," warm spring, or light-bright.

adjusting your colors

If by now you are thoroughly confused and frustrated because you did not find your category, take heart. You may not fit neatly into a season. Remember that we all have our own formulas? You will fit more into one than another, but your fit may not be tidy and neat. You may be one of those lucky people who can wear a lot of colors well. None may jump out as being that much better than others. Usually, persons with a predominance of carotene ("springs" and "autumns") will wear more colors better than those of us with a greater quantity of oxyhemoglobin ("summers" and "winters"). If you are still ignoring all warnings and soaking up the summer sun, or if you think back to when you used to tan, you will notice or remember that you can wear colors with a tan that wouldn't work at all without one. Melanin caused your tan appearance. And melanin is a yellow-brown hue. "Summers" and "winters" become peachier with a tan. The warm browns and yellows that caused your rosy untanned skin to look lined or blotchy will work much better with your tanned skin.

If you still feel confused, you may want to find a qualified color analyst to help you discover your best colors. The analyst can increase your awareness of color and expand the consciousness that you have begun to expand by using this book.

Don't worry. You won't have to throw out all your present clothes. Approximately 75 percent of the clothes in your closet are colors that work well on you. Research by Ameritone Paint shows that by the

Lo and behold, the red sweater looks terrible!

time we are in our early teens, when we are making a lot of important decisions about ourselves, we have begun choosing to wear yellow-based or blue-based colors. And the warmth or coolness of colors is the most important of all the color considerations. Also, our research has shown that 86 percent of us are accurate in our selection of yellow or blue-based colors and that 70 percent of us are also accurate in our choice of clear versus muted colors.

As you buy new clothes, keep in mind the information in this chapter. Within approximately three years, you will have a closet full of your colors. Your shopping will be made easier by knowing which colors are best on you. You will know what to look for and what to avoid. You will save time and energy by eliminating the rack of warm browns if you know none of them will work. And, you won't waste money buying the wonderful camel blazer that you will never wear because it yellows your skin.

Say you decide you look good in red, and you run out to the store to buy that wonderful red sweater you have visualized. You get the sweater home, put it on and, lo and behold, it looks terrible—not wonderful. What went wrong? The key is that all reds are not the same. If you wear cool colors better and the red of your sweater is a warm, fire engine red, you will have a problem. If you wear muted colors, and your sweater is a vibrant clear red, it will not work for you. If you wear low contrast, and you put on a stark white blouse under the sweater, this will be part of the problem. Does the red almost match your hair but is a little bit off? The eye is often disturbed by a combination of two colors that look like they are supposed to match, but they don't quite make it. Determine what colors you don't like to see together. The color wheel "Color Vocabulary," and "Combining Colors Harmoniously" box may be helpful here.

A point to remember: When you are selecting plaid or print clothing to wear near your face, don't necessarily pick out all the individual colors and say: "This has my blue, red, and yellow in it. It will work on me." Rather, squint at the overall clothing piece. What color does it read? Do the red and yellow together read out orange? Do you look good in orange?

♀ colors of makeup

Your body pigmentation is an important factor in choosing makeup. If your skin's undertone is blue, you will wear cool colors best. THINK ROSE. You will wear warmer colors if your skin has a yellow undertone. THINK PEACH.

Squint at a print or plaid to see if the blend of colors reads as a color that will look good on you.

COMBINING COLORS HARMONIOUSLY

1. True (direct) complements (yellow, violet)
2. Split complements (blue, yellow-orange, red-orange)
3. Triad: three colors equidistant on the color wheel (blue, yellow, red)
4. Double complements (blue, orange, violet, yellow)
5. Alternate complements: triad and complement of one (blue, yellow, red, orange)
6. Color analogy: 3 to 6 adjacent colors (blue-violet, violet, red-violet, red)
7. Monochromatic: tints and tones of the same color family (baby blue, medium blue, navy blue)
8. Color apathy: muted, gray, or neutral background with small areas of colors (Chinese art, elementary school drawings)
9. Red, white, blue
10. Cool, clear (cobalt blue and primary red)
11. Cool, muted (denim blue, dusty rose)
12. Warm, clear (orange and crayon yellow)
13. Warm, muted (rust and salmon)
14. Neutrals (cream, rust, and gray)

Makeup

	BLUE-BASED COOL	YELLOW-BASED WARM
Foundation	Rose-beige tones Clove	Cream Bronze Peach Caramel Ivory-peach tones
Blush	Rose family Burgundy Blue-pinks and reds Cherry Plum	Peach family Rust Yellow-pinks and reds Ginger Mocha
Lipstick	Rose family Pink Plums Grape Burgundy Blue-pinks and reds Rosey beige	Peach family Coral Orange Black Honey Poppy Yellow-pinks and reds Rusts, bronzes, coppers

Makeup

	BLUE-BASED COOL	YELLOW-BASED WARM
Nail Polish	Natural Rose family Burgundy Blue-pinks and reds Ruby	Natural Peach family Coral Yellow-pinks and reds Gold
Eye Makeup		
Mascara	Brown Black	Brown Black
Eyebrow	Black Gray taupe Brown-black	Brown Sandy taupe Light brown
Eyeliner	Neutral version of eye color	Neutral version of eye color
Shadow	Grays Gray-blue Blue velvet Plum Mauve Smoked blue-turquoise	Green Brown Mink Cream and beige Apricot Warm turquoise

hair colors

Hair color changes should also be tied to your body pigmentation.

Hair

BLUE-BASED	YELLOW-BASED
Frost with white (ash) tones	Frost with golden tones
Blue-black	Golden brown or blonde
Blue-gray	Warm gray
Ash brown/blonde	Auburn
White	Red
Platinum	Strawberry
Black-brown	Warm dark brown
Black	Flaxen
	Black

jewelry colors

For jewelry, warmer metals and stone colors will work well on warm-toned skins, while silver metals and cool-colored stones work well on blue-based skins.

Jewelry

BLUE-BASED	YELLOW-BASED
Silver	Brass
Platinum	Copper
Rose or cool golds	Yellow gold
White metals	Peach or brown cameos
Rosy hued pearls	Golden hued pearls
Diamonds	Jade
Cool-colored stones	Warm-colored stones
Amethyst	Coral
Rose or white ivory	Tourmaline
Carnelian	Yellow turquoise
Citrine	Amber
Ruby	Topaz . . .
Rose quartz . . .	

You may choose the color of your eyeglass frames to match your hair or skin color. Keep in mind nothing too yellow for blue-based skin, or too rosy for yellow-based skin.

color names

Color names are deceiving. If you tell us you need a white shirt, will that "white" be the same color in our minds as it is in yours? What do you see when you picture teal, taupe, or tawny? Keeping in mind the inaccuracies of color names, let us list some color names that work best with various pigmentations.

Color names

BLUE-BASED CLEAR	BLUE-BASED MUTED	YELLOW-BASED CLEAR	YELLOW-BASED MUTED
NEUTRALS			
White	Winter white	Cinnamon	Cinnamon
Pearl gray	Off white	Acorn	Acorn
Neutral gray	Light, pearl gray	Ecru	Ecru
		Cream	Cream

Color names

BLUE-BASED CLEAR	BLUE-BASED MUTED	YELLOW-BASED CLEAR	YELLOW-BASED MUTED
NEUTRALS *(continued)*			
Gun metal	Rose beige or	Ivory	Ivory
Charcoal	brown	Chamois	Chamois
Black	Cocoa	Champagne	Champagne
Taupe	Pewter	Cappuccino	Cappuccino
Navy	Navy	Rust	Rust
Mineral	Stone	Toffee	Toffee
Graphite		Bronze	Bronze
Black forest		Copper	Copper
		Russet	Russet
		Ginger	Ginger
		Tawny	Tawny
		Camel	Camel
		Mocha	Beige
		Beige	Gold
		Gold	Tan
		Tan	Olive
		Warm gray	Chocolate
			Walnut
			Sable
GREEN			
Jade	Jade	Lime	Nile
Crayon green	Blue-green	Nile	Avocado
Emerald	Smokey green	Apple	Olive
Hunter green	Moss	Citron	Forest green
	Balsam	Crayon green	Herb
	Seafoam	Kelly	Cedar
	Spruce	Chartreuse	Heather
	Sage	Celery	greens
	Heathered		
	greens		
BLUE			
Navy	Navy	Navy	Teal
Powder blue	Powder blue	Aqua	Heathered
Pastel blue	Cool turquoise	Pastel blue	warm blues
Peacock	Peacock	Powder blue	
Azure	Azure	Royal	
Flag	Sapphire	Warm	
Royal	Medium blue	turquoise	
Indigo		Periwinkle	

Color names

BLUE-BASED CLEAR	BLUE-BASED MUTED	YELLOW-BASED CLEAR	YELLOW-BASED MUTED
BLUE *(continued)* Sapphire Icy blue Chinese blue Cobalt	Denim blue China Ash blue-green Smoked blue turquoise Periwinkle Heathered cool blues		
PURPLE Iris Blue purple Plum Wisteria Wineberry Lilac Lavender Laurel Violet	Plum Eggplant Wisteria Aubergene Gray-purple mauve Grape Heathered cool violets	None	Muted, warm violet Eggplant Aubergine Heathered warm violets
YELLOW Primary yellow Lemon	Butter yellow	Primary yellow Lemon Canary Buttercup Yellow-orange Buddha gold Clear, desert gold Marigold Bright gold	Gold Topaz Pale honey
ORANGE None	Cool coral	Tangerine Peach Poppy Coral Apricot Bittersweet	Salmon Pumpkin Smokey coral Ginger Bittersweet Brick

Color names

BLUE-BASED CLEAR	BLUE-BASED MUTED	YELLOW-BASED CLEAR	YELLOW-BASED MUTED
RED			
Dubonnet	Cranberry	Cardinal	Brick
Cranberry	Pink orchid	Crimson	Salmon
Blush rose	Pastel pink	Tangerine	Smokey coral
Cardinal	Blush rose	Fire engine red	Bittersweet
Cerise	Watermelon red	Primary red	
Bright pink	Blue-pink	Peach	
Crimson	Barely pink	Poppy	
Burgundy	Raspberry	Coral	
Wine		Apricot	
Primary red		Bittersweet	
Barely pink		Orange red	
Ruby		Chinese red	
Merlot			

Besides *body pigmentation,* you also will want to consider six other points as you select the colors you wear.

1. *What colors do you like?* We all have different backgrounds, and our past experience with colors affects which colors we prefer. Dr. Max Luscher and Faber Berren, both respected colorists, have reported the following pleasant and unpleasant associations people have with various colors.[1]

Color association chart

COLOR	PLEASANT ASSOCIATIONS	UNPLEASANT ASSOCIATIONS
Red	exciting, stimulating, loving, powerful, strong, warm, human	aggressive, disturbing, vulgar, bloody, defiant
Orange	friendly, jovial, incandescent, social	intrusive, gaudy, blustering
Yellow	sunny, cheerful, optimistic, expansive, radiant	glaring, imperious, bilious, eccentric
Green	tranquil, quiet, consoling, comforting, natural	commonplace, tiresome

Color association chart

COLOR	PLEASANT ASSOCIATIONS	UNPLEASANT ASSOCIATIONS
Blue	calm, comfortable, secure	depressing, melancholy, lonely, cold
Indigo	royal, deep, calm	heavy, dark, lonely
Violet	regal, exclusive, dignified	conceited, funereal, esoteric, pompous
White	innocent, hopeful, celestial, spiritual	sterile, glaring, unemotional, bleak
Gray	secure, peaceful, protective, safe	dreary, tedious, passive, negative, colorless
Black	sophisticated	deathly, ominous, empty, fatal
Brown	dependable, steady, reliable	clumsy, boring, dour, stingy, obstinate
Pink	dainty, sweet, gentle, tender	effete, effeminate, saccharine

Look back to Chapter 1 (question 66) for women and Chapter 2 (question 74 for men). Note which colors you associated with adjectives that you don't want associated with you? It is important for you to remember that even though pink may do wonderful things for your skin, if your mind associates it with weakness and you want to appear powerful, you won't want to wear pink.

2. What is your *personality type*? Are you shy and like to fade into the background? Even if you look great in orange, people will notice you when you wear it. So don't wear it, especially on those days you're feeling especially vulnerable. If you are on a panel and are not prepared for your portion of the discussion, don't wear crayon red even though it may do wonderful things for your coloring. You may not normally be shy, but you will want to blend in on this particular day.

3. What parts of your *body* do you want to accentuate? If you decided you look great in vivid, clear yellow, and you have large hips, you will not want to wear yellow on your hips. Light, bright, warm,

You can lift your spirits and those of others by wearing bright colors on gloomy days.

clear colors advance. They make you look larger. If your shoulders and torso are small in comparison to your hips, you will want to wear a yellow shirt or jacket to increase the size of your torso. Then your torso will balance your hips. You could wear dark, dull, cool, or muted pants because these colors recede. They make you appear smaller.

Remember from Chapter 5, color carries the eye. So use advancing colors (light, bright, warm, or clear) to take the eye to your body assets, for example, a tan belt on a small waist, a red tie near your brilliant "words," wine nail polish on pretty hands.

4. What is the *weather* today? Weather is important in color selection. Blue-based, light colors are cooler, while yellow-based, dark colors are warmer. Black is hot in the summer because it absorbs the light, while white is cool because it reflects light.

On a dreary day, do you tend to reach for dreary-colored clothing? You can lift your spirits and those of others by wearing your yellow, red, or orange on those gloomy days. Bright colors brighten gloomy days!

5. What are your *best neutrals*? If neutrals make up the backbone of your wardrobe, you will get away with fewer clothes because neutrals are forgettable colors. You can wear the same navy blue suit a couple of days of the same week and people will not realize that you have done so. Neutrals go with nearly everything. The best neutrals for our varying pigmentations are in the chart below.

Neutrals

BLUE-BASED CLEAR	BLUE-BASED MUTED	YELLOW-BASED CLEAR	YELLOW-BASED MUTED
Pure white	Rose brown or	Ivory	Ivory
Navy	rose beige	Navy	Chocolate brown
Burgundy	Winter white	Rust	Rust
Gray	Burgundy	Camel	Camel
Hunter green	Blue-gray	Beige	Beige
Black	Navy	Gold	Gold
Taupe		Tan	Tan
		Warm gray	Bronze
			Forest green
			Olive
			Teal
			Brick

6. What *messages* do your colors send? A dark suit and light shirt, e.g., navy with white is a *powerful* color combination. They announce that you are in control, that you have authority. *Presence* colors call attention to you. The message you send when you wear a plum blouse with your navy suit or a white tie with a black shirt is "notice me." In the business world, color is a good way for women to call attention to themselves in an asexual way. There's no need to wear the skirt slit to the hip or the blouse unbuttoned to the navel. A *friendly* color combination is your beige, khaki, tan, or camel jacket with a pale blue shirt. Also, navy with pale yellow sends the message, "I am in a good mood."

Neutrals are upper-class colors and are often worn together (e.g., camel jacket with navy, black, or gray slacks.) Because lower-class, less expensive clothing has been made from lavender, gold, mustard, and green, it has not tested well in the business world. If you buy an exquisitely designed lavender silk shirt, you will probably do fine, but keep in mind the message lavender sends to many people. You may not want to wear lavender the day you are giving a speech or leading a meeting. Bright and light suits and multicolored shoes have not worked well at work. They send a "going to the club" or "going out to lunch" message.

Keeping the above information in mind, you can have fun with colors. Begin by breaking habits. Try different colors together. Experiment and be creative! *Dress Smart* by wearing colors that work for you.

review

What do you remember about this chapter that is significant to *you*? First, list surprises, "ahas," lightbulbs in the page of your journal that follows. Then, look back through this chapter and list those discoveries you want to highlight.

● ●

Review: chapter 6

"Ahas"

1. _____

_____

2. _____

_____

3. _____

_____

Discoveries to highlight

_____

_____

_____

_____

_____

_____

_____

_____

● ●

The review page at the end of this chapter will be useful later as you want to review *Dress Smart*. You won't need to reread the chapter, just your "ahas."

endnote

1. Copyright © 1979 *Glamour*, Condé Nast Publications Inc. Reprinted by permission. All rights reserved. Courtesy of Dr. Max Luscher and Faber Birren.

use the modular approach to wardrobe building

7

Just think how nice it would be to wake up in the morning, reach into the closet, and pull out something you really love.

We don't need an abundance of clothes. In fact, our lives would be made much simpler if we had fewer decisions to make regarding clothing. Just think how nice it would be to wake up in the morning, reach into the closet, and pull out something you really loved to wear. And then to pull out a second item which works well with the first. Every item you pulled out would be just right for you.

Unfortunately that's probably not how it is! Chances are that although your closet is stuffed, your wardrobe is limited. It is estimated that we invest an average of $3,000 in our wardrobes, but we wear only 10 percent of what we own. The solution? Using *Dress Smart*, learn why the 90 percent of your clothing that doesn't work, doesn't work. Learn not to make those same mistakes again. Then get everything out of your closet that doesn't make you feel your best. Keep only workable, wonderful clothing in the closet. That will simplify your life!

How do we build a wardrobe that works together and does great things for us in a minimum of time? How do we cut down on the number of clothing items in our closet while increasing our number of outfits?

Let's begin by studying the Women's Modular Outfits on the following two pages. Count the number of clothing items represented.

limiting your color choices

One principal to remember in our quest to simplify our wardrobes is to limit our choices to two or three basic colors, usually neutrals, and colors that go with them. In Chapter 6, you discovered your best neutrals, those forgettable colors you can wear several times a week and no one notices. Check the ones that are yours in your

Modular outfits.

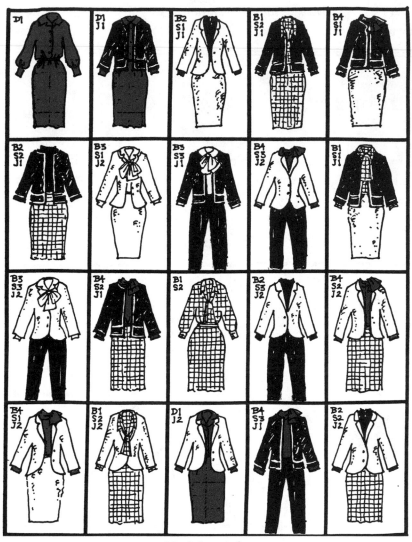

Modular outfits.

journal. Then, go to your closet and pull out your favorite outfits and clothing items—those things that make you feel and look wonderful—and complete the chart.

● ● ● ● ● ● ● ● ● ● ● ● ● ● ● ● ● ● ●

Your neutral colors

black   _____

white   _____

gray   _____

navy   _____

brown   _____

burgundy   _____

forest/hunter green   _____

teal   _____

beige   _____

taupe   _____

camel   _____

rust   _____

other   _____

● ●

Wonderful colors

Outfits/clothing items   *colors*

1. _____

2. _____

3. _____

_____

_____

● ●

If none are neutral in color, maybe you are a person who does not want to blend in. Are you a person who usually wears bright and unusual colors? People will remember if you wear a red suit twice in one week. You will not be able to repeat that outfit often. You will need more clothes if you build around nonneutrals, but you may choose to do just that. Those wonderful clothing items may also be wonderful because of something more than color, such as the fit, fabric or design. Most likely if you love certain clothes, they will also love you. Think about why you love your favorite clothes. Then make a list of the basic colors around which you want to build your wardrobe and another list for your appropriate accent colors.

● ●

My basic colors

1. _____

2. _____

3. _____

● ●

My accent colors

1. _____

2. _____

3. _____

4. _____

5. _____

6. _____

7. _____

8. _____

9. _____

10. _____

11. _____

12. _____

● ●

The list of accent colors could go on and on, especially if your basic colors are neutrals. Neutrals go well with many colors!

If you look back to Chapter 6 at the ways to combine colors harmoniously, you will remember that the main pitfall in putting colors together is trying to combine colors that look like they are supposed to match, but are a little bit off. You can tie most colors together by bringing the bottom color up (e.g. pant color in a tie). Think of many possibilities when you think of accents. But don't use too many accents at once! Be creative. Challenge your assumptions.

creating a modular wardrobe

Back to our question on page 175. Did you determine that there were ten clothing items involved in that module? If so, you were correct.

The pictured wardrobe is called a Modular Wardrobe. It is a good place to begin when building a woman's basic wardrobe. Janet Wallach discusses the same basic idea as the Capsule Concept in her book *Working Wardrobe*. The basic wardrobe concept is nothing new. It goes way back in history. The modular format is a simple way of looking at the basic wardrobe: 1, 2, 3, 4. These numbers form a pyra-

A modular wardrobe for women.

A modular wardrobe for men.

mid of clothing items for women: 1 dress, 2 jackets, 3 bottoms, and 4 tops make forty nonrepeated outfits. That is eight weeks of five working days each. And in all but thirteen of the forty days, the outfits contain jackets, the major authority component of career apparel. Notice that all clothing items go together. They are in the same mood and are made of patterns and textures that work together.

We can easily apply this modular concept to the male context. For men: 1 sport jacket, 2 pair of trousers, 3 suits, and 6 tops give you similar flexibility.

As you buy your apparel, think double duty. Visually take apart a suit and see it as separates: the jacket as a sportcoat and the trouser or skirt as worn with other separates. Remember though, YOU MUST ALWAYS CLEAN BOTH PARTS OF YOUR SUIT TO-GETHER, so they will continue to match and work together. Yes, this means you clean the bottom if you've only worn it one time and you have just spilled coffee on its matching jacket. This principal also applies to blouses with detachable matching ties and sweater sets. Wash both parts together so they will continue to work as a set.

Be certain that the basic components of your modular wardrobe are classics if you want to get the most mileage out of your clothing. (You can always update with props and accessories.)

defining classics

At least *some* grandmothers could have worn *some* classic clothing.

What are the classics anyway? Classic is defined as "of the highest rank, of the first order . . . approved as a model, standard, leading."

The classic look is timeless. Classic clothing could have been worn by our grandmothers, and they would have looked fine. Today we can wear a classic suit and look grand, even though all our friends are wearing the latest width lapels and skirt lengths. Holly Brubach wrote in the May 1984 *Atlantic* magazine: "Classic clothes have an air of superiority about them, partly because they're the clothes most worn by rich people and partly because they profess in immunity to the whims and longings that come over the rest of us. It's as if the world were a giant emporium, with a little balcony where the sensible few in their classic clothes sit and watch the fashion-conscious masses in their platform shoes and shoulder pads come and go beneath them."[1]

Some classic guidelines

CLOTHING	DESCRIPTION
1. Lapel	$3^1/_4$–$3^1/_2$ inches
2. Shirt collar	$3^1/_4$–$3^1/_2$ inches
3. Sleeve	► Set in ► Gathered to cuff or medium-width band ► Medium gathers ► Hemmed with narrow hem
4. Cuffs on sleeves	$1^1/_4$ inches
5. Waistband	$1^1/_4$ inches
6. Cuffs on trousers	$1^1/_4$ inches

Some classic guidelines

CLOTHING	DESCRIPTION
7. Belt loops	$^1/_4$ inches
8. Skirt	▸ Length, 3 fingers below kneecap ▸ Lower edge 40–50 inches wide ▸ Straight, pleated, dirndl, A-line
9. Pants	▸ With or without cuffs ▸ End at top of shoe in front and slant to midpoint of heel in back ▸ Straight or slightly tapered from knee ▸ Fly front
10. Coats	▸ Wrap (polo) ▸ Trench—double- or single-breasted ▸ Single-breasted with notch collar ▸ Double-breasted ▸ Princess line ▸ Chanel (cardigan)
11. Evening wear	▸ Tuxedo ▸ Grecian style ▸ Off-shoulder sheath ▸ Spaghetti straps ▸ Strapless ▸ Floor length
12. Fabrics	▸ Linen ▸ Cotton ▸ Wool ▸ Silk ▸ Rayon ▸ Microfiber ▸ Blends ▸ Gabardine ▸ Denim ▸ Crepe ▸ Corduroy ▸ Flannel ▸ Ultra suede ▸ Knits
13. Dresses	▸ Shirt dresses ▸ Sweater dresses ▸ Coat dresses

mix and match quality clothes

If our goal is to simplify our wardrobes so we can get on with doing what is really important in our lives, then we must assemble a wardrobe that works as hard as we do. Start with one module, then add another module later if you wish. And if the two modules work together, just think of all the combinations you can make! If you make the dress in the module a matching skirt and blouse, you have greatly increased the number of outfits. Add a vest that goes with the other ten items and you've increased the number of combinations again. Add a sweater that work with the color, mood, and patterns, and again the number of combinations skyrockets. Men might coordinate a sport coat, sweater, turtleneck, and a cardigan with a single pair of pants! Add braces and a tie for yet another look.

So you don't need a lot of clothes to have a lot of outfits. You don't need QUANTITY. But you do need QUALITY if you want to look successful. And looking successful is the first step to being successful. Buy clothing with quality design, quality line, quality workmanship, quality color, and quality fiber. So, remember, *buy fewer, but better clothes*! Never buy junk.

"But," you say, "I can't afford quality clothing. Most of my money goes for my car, housing, food, and entertainment," You are partly right. Quality clothing is not cheap! Unless you are an easy-to-fit size and are skilled at shopping sales or discount houses, you will need to spend money to acquire quality clothing. *But, you are worth it*! Many of us have inherited depression-era thinking. Many of our mothers or grandmothers never spent money on themselves. But we need to think of it this way: We can leave our cars and our homes behind, but we take ourselves with us wherever we go. We must put planning and necessary money into our clothing because we are never separated from our clothing (except in our worst nightmares!) and we are constantly judged by the way we look. You can't afford *not* to wear quality! Our clothing makes a statement, so let it say "I am a success." There is no such thing as neutral clothing!

One consolation is that we don't need a lot to make a lot. We need to put the largest amount of money into our suits, if we are in careers that require suits. And if we buy one good, classic suit per season, we will soon have accumulated enough to give us the variety to build one or more modules.

It has been said that all problems could be handled if we could change our point of view. So, let's look at our clothing as an *investment* rather than as an *expense*. Let's handle the money problem by considering the cost-per-wear. To figure the cost-per-wear, divide the cost of the item by the number of times you anticipate that item will be worn in its lifetime.

If we are lucky, we are never separated from our clothing.

Let's look at two classic navy blue blazers. Both are made of year-round fabrics, and both can be worn twice a week because they are a neutral color and go with all our other wardrobe items. One costs $400, and the other costs $160. The $400 blazer should last five years or more, whereas the $160 blazer will be wearable for one year. The cost-per-wear for the $400 blazer would be half as much as the $160 blazer:

$$\frac{\$400}{520 \text{ wears}} = \$.80 \qquad \frac{\$160}{104 \text{ wears}} = \$1.60$$

Which one would you buy? If we want to look successful, we buy quality. And if we amortize the cost, it becomes easier to justify the expenditure. In contrast, what would the cost-per-wear be for the $800 high-fashion, fuchsia dress that you could wear only three times because it soon is out of style or is so unique that everyone remembers it when you wear it?

recognizing quality

How can you recognize quality when you see it? Is a $400 suit automatically of better quality than a $160 one? Some people spend a lot of money on their clothes, but never look put-together. Others spend much less, but use good taste to turn out a finished look. If quality has not been a part of your history, one way to discover what quality is all about is to use the cross-shopping method.

Go to a store which carries expensive clothing. Which stores in your city carry expensive clothes? Ask around to get store names if necessary. Then, dress nicely and walk into the store as if you belonged. Examine different clothing items closely. Look at the seams, look at the design, look at the buttons, stitching, and details. Record your observations.

● ●

Expensive clothing

Local stores

_____

_____

_____

_____

_____

Observations of quality

_____

_____

_____

_____

_____

_____

● ●

Now, go to a store that carries low-priced garments or to the budget department of a department store. Examine clothing items as carefully as you did in the high-priced store. Note your observations below.

● ●

Observations of inexpensive clothing

_____

_____

_____

● ●

Did you discover that quality items possess these qualities?

1. Generous even seams (1/2 inch) and hem allowances ($1^1/_4$–$2^1/_2$ inch)
2. Top stitching even and straight, 15 stitches per inch
3. No strings hanging
4. Dart tips smooth, not puckered
5. Shoulder seams straight, no puckers
6. Sleeves not skimpy
7. Hem even, stitching invisible from outside
8. Lining fits, is of good fabric
9. Zipper color matches fabric exactly, opens and closes easily
10. Buttonholes evenly spaced, stitched neatly
11. Wood, metal, bone, pearl buttons; shank buttons on coats

12. No pulling of fabric

13. Wrinkles disappear quickly when fabric is squeezed, held, and released

14. When held to the light, fabric shows no thin areas

15. Fabric feels like a natural fiber

16. The more expensive the garment, the smaller size you wear!

17. No plastic thread

Go to a bookstore or magazine stand and look at the clothing ads and other clothing photographs in the *New York Times Sunday Magazine*. Check out *W, Women's Wear Daily*, and *Town and Country*. Wealthy, well-bred people seem to be in quality clothing which appears to be made of cotton, wool, silk, linen, leather, suede, or fur. What do cotton, wool, silk, linen, leather, suede, or fur have in common? They are all natural materials. Natural materials look rich. These materials and the new microfiber synthetics that look natural have advantages over the old plasticlike or flimsy synthetics. Because they breathe, they are cooler in the summer and warmer in the winter. They don't stain permanently. They don't need a lot of cleaning. In fact, by airing out a wool suit in a steamy bathroom and brushing it occasionally, it can go nearly a whole winter without dry cleaning. Of course this would not be the care required for those of us who sweat profusely, or those of us who are clumsy with our food and drink. But most Americans tend to overclean. What we do by frequent cleaning is shorten the life of our garments. We overwork the fibers. Hang your wrinkled wool garment over a tub of steaming water, close the shower curtain and the bathroom door, and presto—you get a smooth garment that also smells fresh.

And there are products that freshen up your garments. Check out sprays and dryer additives in the laundry section of your grocery store. Another care tip for natural materials is to let them sit between wearings (e.g., rotate your leather shoes, don't wear that blazer Monday and Tuesday, but Monday and Wednesday).

Many people do not want to wear something pretending to be cotton (or pretending to be *anything* for that matter!) when they can have the real thing. They believe in the integrity of the material. You will have to decide how you feel about this. In Chapter 1 or Chapter 2, you asked yourself if you are willing to iron cotton or to clean silk. Check back to page 20 for women or 53 for men if you need to review your reaction to various fabrics. If you are not willing to look a bit crumpled occasionally, you will not be comfortable in some natural fibers. But to get the quality look if you won't wear natural fibers, you must select blends or synthetics that LOOK LIKE NATURAL FIBERS. Again, you may need to cross-shop. What does

Give your wool garments a treat.

a silk blouse look like? Which polyester or blends have that real silk look?

Synthetics are constantly being improved. Today there is much less pilling and snagging than even five years ago. And synthetics do strengthen the natural fiber with which they are blended. They also add wrinkle resistance. There are benefits to blends, but never forget that the successful, quality look is the natural fiber.

Keep in mind that research shows that some natural fibers don't work well in a conservative *business* setting. Linen can become overly wrinkled. Suede, leather, fur, and velvet can carry negative connotations, and corduroy can appear too casual. You will have to decide which fabrics lend themselves to your image and lifestyle.

review

What do you remember about this chapter that is significant to *you*? First, list surprises, "ahas," lightbulbs in the page of your journal that follows. Then, look back through this chapter and list those discoveries you want to highlight.

Linen can become very wrinkled and look inappropriate in a business setting.

● ● ● ● ● ● ● ● ● ● ● ● ● ● ● ● ● ● ●

Review: chapter 7

"Ahas"

1. _____

_____

2. _____

_____

3. _____

_____

Discoveries to highlight

_____

_____

_____

_____

_____

_____

The review page at the end of this chapter will be useful later as you want to review *Dress Smart*. You won't need to reread the chapter, just your "ahas."

endnote

1. Holly Brubach, "The Truth in Fiction," *The Atlantic*, May, 1984.

consider the total look

8

It is important to attend to all details when you dress. It is equally important to get out of the way you look and into the world around you.

Do you know the woman who is always combing her hair, or the man who is always checking himself out as he passes a mirror? That person is most likely insecure about the way he or she looks. Have you ever felt insecure about the way you looked? What steps can you take to change self-consciousness to self-confidence? What do you need to be able to waltz past a mirror without a glance, knowing you look great? Would it help to know what is expected of well-dressed people?

Let's go head to toe and examine all details. To begin, you'll need a full-length mirror hung in a well-lit spot near your clothing.

We will examine:

Head
Chest
Waist
Hands, hips, legs
Feet
Backview
Everything else

examine yourself

Use the following "Total Look" chart to examine yourself for what you now think is dressing smart. Check under column 1 all the parts you think *need work*. (You will work with the rest of the columns at the end of the chapter.)

● ●

Total look exercise

Today do you want to look _____ authoritative _____ approachable?

	7	6	5	4	3	2	1
Head							
1. Hair							
a. clean							
b. combed							
c. cut							
d. color							
e. style							
f. on face							
2. Glasses							
a. shape							
b. scale							
c. color							
d. style							
e. fit							
3. Skin care							
4. Makeup in general							
5. Eyes							

	7	6	5	4	3	2	1
6. Cheeks							
7. Lips							
8. Cover-up							
9. Foundation							
10. Eyebrows							
11. Powder							
12. Earrings							
13. Hats							
a. color							
b. style							
c. scale							
d. fabric							
14. Smoking							
15. Mouth							
a. teeth							
b. breath							
c. gum							
16. Jewelry							
17. Neck							
Chest							
1. Jacket—If none, should there be today?							
a. lapel							
b. vent							
c. button							
d. sleeve length							
e. jacket length							
f. color							

	7	6	5	4	3	2	I
g. fabric							
h. fit							
i. style							
2. Shirt/Sweater							
a. collar							
b. cuff							
c. buttons							
d. sleeve length							
e. monogram							
f. color							
g. fabric							
h. fit							
i. style							
3. Pocket handkerchief							
4. Tie or scarf—If none, should there be today?							
a. pattern							
b. length							
c. width							
d. color							
e. material							
5. Lapel pin							
Waist							
1. Belt							
a. buckle							
b. placement							
c. color							
d. material							

	7	6	5	4	3	2	I
Hands, Hips, & Legs							
1. Nails							
2. Jewelry							
3. Pants							
a. length							
b. cuffed or not							
c. width							
d. color							
e. fabric							
f. fit							
g. style							
4. Skirt							
a. length							
b. color							
c. fabric							
d. fit							
e. style							
Feet							
1. Shoes							
a. polished							
b. heels							
c. color							
d. material							
e. fit							
f. style							
2. Socks/Hose							
a. color							
b. fabric							

	7	6	5	4	3	2	I
c. fit							
d. style							
Backview							
Everything else							
1. Fragrance							
2. Matching or coordinating							
3. Authoritative vs. approachable							
4. Patterns appropriate							
5. Coat							
6. Briefcase/Purse							
7. Props							
a. pen							
b. notebook							
c. umbrella							
d. wallet							
e. calendar							
f. palm pilot							
g. calculator							
h. checkbook							
i. computer							
j. cell phone							
k. beeper							
l. coinpurse							
m. pill case							
n. key case							
o. sunglasses							

	7	6	5	4	3	2	1
p. recorder/CD player							
q. car							
r. office							
s. home							
t. memos							
u. other							
8. Dress (rate as skirt and shirt)							
9. Underwear							

examine the details

Next, let's learn the details, head to toe. Skip over the parts that don't apply.

Study yourself head to toe

HEAD

1. Hair
   - *Clean*
   - *Great cut*—your styling preference and suited to your facial type
   - *Classic style*—Works best for business—Not dated: many of us keep those styles we had in an important part of our lives (e.g. when we met our husband, when we were with a rock band, when we were valedictorian or beauty queen).
   - *Well combed*
   - *Easy-care style*—If we are in business, we need to be perceived as not needing to spend too much time on make-up or hair. Otherwise we can be perceived as a lightweight, with vanity taking priority over job.
   - *Fidget proof*—Playing with hair is viewed as a sexual or nervous gesture
   - *Pulled back*—if longer than your shoulders, when you go to work
   - *Natural-looking color*—nothing too garish, too dark, or too brassy. Women looking for a job in business have more credibility and authority if

A great haircut is a priority.

they do not have gray hair. As unfair as it is, women have not been viewed as wise, distinguished people when hair begins to silver, but sometimes as old women. This is changing with the graying of America, but meanwhile it is good to be aware. Nongray hair can give the illusion of youth. And if we choose to color our hair, lighter is better than darker. Because our skin becomes thinner and more delicately colored as we get older, it is easily overpowered by dark-colored hair. And of course any colored hair will want to look like you didn't color it. For men, gray hair is just fine.

▶ *Thinning hair*—can be helped by products on the market and a good cut.

▶ *Balding head*—inevitable for some. A very short haircut or shaved head can look "with it." Definitely don't try the comb over.

▶ *Facial hair, women*—If you have a mustache or other facial hair, you may consider *electrolysis* or facial *waxing*.

▶ *Facial hair, men*—If you have a beard or mustache, keep it well groomed. Is the style appropriate for you and your workplace? What message is it sending? Often times people react to beards as they do to sunglasses: they're scared of what's behind them.

2. Glasses ▶ *Facial shape*:

Square face—Don't wear square glasses unless you want to emphasize your square face. Round glasses work well.

Round face—Don't wear round glasses unless you want to emphasize your round face. Oval glasses work well.

Long, thin face—You can widen the look of your face with wide glasses.

Heart-shaped face—De-emphasize the wideness of the forehead by avoiding heart shaped or triangular lenses.

▶ *Scale*—Fine-pointed or delicate features will not look good with chunky glasses. Large-featured persons look silly in fragile glasses.

▶ *Balance*—Although you may not want to emphasize a facial line by repeating it, you will want to add quantity to the eye area if your jaw is large. If you have a dominant square chin, you might like large and round glasses.

For a heart-shaped face, glasses that are narrow across the forehead will deemphasize wideness.

▶ *Color*—For an unobtrusive pair of glasses, match your skin or hair or wear a no-frame pair. Heavy, dark frames for business can add authority to a small face if authority is important to you. You may choose to wear heavy dark-framed glasses for work even though a different style and color would be more flattering. If you tint your glasses, don't go too dark on the tint. You can also wear frames of your colors or metals. Don't keep sunglasses on at work. People feel uncomfortable when they can't see your eyes.

▶ Beware of glasses with photo sensitive lenses for photographs! They will be darker in the photograph. Substitute another pair when taking a picture.

▶ *Style*—You may want to choose glasses as your signature and do something all your own. What about half glasses if you only need them for reading? Match the style of your glasses to your personal style. For instance, a tinted frame with jewels would seem inappropriate for a NATURAL type personality. Also, that frame might work at the opera but look silly on the sailboat. If you can no longer find the style you have always worn, you may want to switch and move on or perhaps if they are your style statement, you will have to search harder.

▶ *Simplicity of line*—Usually less is more. Designer's initials are a turn-off for a lot of people. Too much embellishment does not look like quality.

Usually less is more. Too much embellishment does not look like quality.

> ▶ *Good fit advice*—Classic glasses rest on the bridge of your nose and not on your cheek bones.
>
> ▶ Decide how to keep your glasses *safe* when they are not being worn: attractive case, chain, or inside jacket pocket. Whatever works efficiently, do. No fumbling.

3. Skin Care

> ▶ *Healthy*, glowing skin is a goal at any age. Start with a gentle cleanser followed by a clarifier for ph balance and a moisturizer at *bedtime* and in the *morning*.
>
> ▶ Find a regimen that works for your skin type.
>
> ▶ Exfoliant scrubs or hydroxy creams help remove sluffed cells from older skin.

4. Makeup in general

> ▶ *Suited to activity and personal style*—Natural for a sporting event; not contrived if you are a natural type; never overdone for business. It could look like you spent more time preparing your face than preparing for the meeting!
>
> ▶ *Emphasize your best assets*
>
> ▶ *Balance is classic*: Is your lipstick too dark for your eyes?

5. Eyes

> ▶ *Natural-looking* mascara
>
> ▶ *Separated lashes* (wait until mascara dries if you add another coat)
>
> ▶ For swimming or if you think your eyes may tear, wear waterproof mascara
>
> ▶ *Natural-colored shadows* for work
>
> ▶ *Continue* shadow up past lid
>
> ▶ *If deep-set eyes*: Use lighter colored shadow to draw your eyelids out (remember light advances). Try pale pink or cream or light gray-blue.
>
> ▶ *If eyes protrude*: Use darker colors to make your lids appear smaller (remember dark recedes). Your eyes will look good lined. Use darker roses, browns, blue or green-gray shadows and dark neutral liners.
>
> ▶ Look back at page 165 in the color chapter and review your best colors of eye makeup. Decide which ones you intend to use.
>
> ▶ Do not keep liquid eye makeup for more than six months as it can breed and spread bacteria.
>
> ▶ If your eyes are sensitive, you should avoid eye makeup or at least look into hypoallergenic brands. Tearing allergic eyes are both troublesome and unattractive.
>
> ▶ *Application Procedure*—A number of procedures are appropriate. We'll share this one with you.

Choose two colors of shadow and place three dots of the darker one as shown. Connect these dots. Apply two dots with lighter shadow (see X at right). Connect these dots. With cotton or a natural-haired brush blend shadows toward your nose. You now have three colors from the use of two shadows

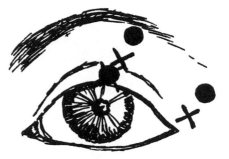

Eye makeup.

6. Cheeks

▸ *Wear blue-based or yellow-based* blush depending on your undertone.

▸ Go no further toward your nose than *mid-eye*.

▸ *Smile* and look in the mirror. See the fat area, the apple? Your blush should add subtle color to this "apple" only.

▸ A good *application* procedure is to place three dots on the "apple" of your cheek and then brush or rub into hair line. Use a tissue to remove any color in the hair.

▸ Keep it *natural* looking—no clown cheeks!

▸ Look at page 163 to determine your best blush colors.

7. Lips

▸ For work, lipstick should be a natural extension of normal lip color—not dark or bright.

▸ *Blue-based* pinks, roses, plums, and reds are colors for summers and winters and *yellow-based* pinks, peaches, corals, and reds are for springs and autumns.

▸ Think about your best lipstick colors (see page 163).

▸ *Frosted lipstick* (or any other makeup for that matter) can look cheap and emphasize lines that increase along with years.

▸ Use *lipliner* in the same or slightly darker color than lipstick for a neat outlined lip. Begin at the corners and work toward the middle, top and bottom lips. If you cover your entire lip with pencil, your lipstick will stay on well, but lipliner is drying to your lips. Using a lip brush will help lipstick stay on. A brush places the lipstick into the lip crevices. If you blot after applying lipstick, powder your lips (baby powder or translucent powder), and reapply lipstick with a brush, your lipstick should stay on very well. Your lipstick will be more colorful and shiny without an overall blot. If you prefer the look of unblotted lipstick, at least blot the inside of your lips (lipstick on teeth is not good looking) and the outer edge of your bottom lip (neither is lipstick on your chin). If you still like a bit of a gloss, add lip gloss. Shiny lips are sexy, so blotting the gloss will make the shine subtle and appropriate for business.

► Remember balance—If your lower lip is larger than your upper, outline the outermost edge of the upper lip and the innermost edge of the bottom. And vice versa. Don't draw on extra lip.

8. Cover-up

► Put cover-up on before foundation.

► Take care with fragile skin under your eyes—use a liquid for this area and pat (don't rub) toward the nose.

► Use a shade lighter than your foundation.

9. Foundation

► Match facial skin color exactly—check out where neck and chin meet.

► Apply lightly and evenly.

► If you are wearing the colors best for your coloring, you may not need foundation. One purpose of foundation is to blend various shades of the face to look one color. Also, foundation serves a protective function. Lightly blend foundation with gravity (downward), especially if you have facial hair. If you have oily skin, use water-based or light, oil-based foundation, and vice versa.

► Blend other makeup against gravity to save sagging skin.

► Use a tissue to remove any foundation which gets into the hairline.

► Blend onto the top of the neck.

10. Eyebrows

► A brush applicator is good for applying liner naturally. Avoid drawn-on brows.

► Match your brow, colorwise. Extend your brow if you can do so naturally so a straight line extends from your nose to the outer corner of your eye to the outer edge of your brow.

► Natural brows may be trimmed and shaped.

► Pluck stray hairs from below your brow and toward your nose. Do not pluck above the brow.

11. Powder

► A large, quality natural-bristled brush or makeup sponge is good for powder. A cotton ball or a pad or a clean puff will also work.

► Use powder to set your makeup when putting it on in the morning or to "deshine" your nose or forehead later in the day.

► Blotting with tissue also works for "deshining."

► Remove extra powder with the "depowdered" brush or cotton.

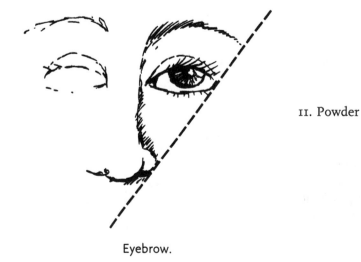

Eyebrow.

12. Earrings

▸ Use translucent or baby powder.

▸ Decide if your earrings are your statement.

▸ Make your earrings subtle for business—small, quality, natural stones, nothing dangling. Do not let them distract from your WORDS.

▸ Many people react negatively to men wearing earrings.

13. Hats

▸ Wear colors that work for you.

▸ Wear styles that accentuate your facial features. If your face is long, avoid narrow-shaped hats. Widen your face with a wide brim. If your face is heart-shaped, pull the eye away from your narrow chin by adding height to the top. Avoid large brims which can make your chin disappear. If your face is wide, wear a narrow-brimmed hat. If your face is round, add length by a hat with a tall crown.

▸ Coordinate the mood of your hat with the occasion (e.g. wear a felt fedora to your bank office rather than a tweedy, racing hat). Neither your "going to tea," nor your ski hats will be appropriate for work.

▸ Size is important—neither too big nor too small for your face/build or the occasion.

14. Smoking

▸ Maybe today is the day for you to quit!

▸ Be certain before you light up that your smoking will not offend anyone.

▸ If you are going to smoke, remember your etiquette:

  ▸ Don't have a cigarette dangling from your lips.

  ▸ Always keep your fingers on the cigarette while lighting it.

  ▸ Don't blow smoke in anyone's face or let the heat vents do it for you.

  ▸ Don't walk carrying a cigarette.

15. Mouth

▸ Floss your teeth daily.

▸ Brush at least twice a day.

▸ When eating, check for "dangling spinach."

▸ Breath spray or mints are handy to have on hand in your briefcase, car, or desk drawer.

▸ Bad breath can be a great liability.

▸ Chew gum only in private, and then with your mouth closed.

16. Jewelry

▸ For the job, do not overdo jewelry of any kind. Minimal jewelry works best: two rings, watch, simple earrings, pearls or gold chain, subtle lapel pin—nothing clanking or distracting.

If your face is long, widen it with a wide-brimmed hat. If your face is short, wear a hat with a narrow brim and full crown.

Bad breath can be a great liability.

▶ Coordinate color of stone and metals with your body color.

▶ If not real stone or metal, be certain it looks real.

▶ Accumulate good jewelry through the years. Ask for it for Christmas or birthdays. Shop for unique jewelry in antique stores and at art museums and galleries.

▶ Decide if certain pieces of jewelry are your signatures.

▶ Consider your colors for your best jewelry colors.

▶ If you are in a creative line of work—art, design, architecture—your jewelry can be individualistic. Still, don't overdo.

▶ Scale your jewelry to you. Let it be in proportion with you.

▶ Don't wear controversial lapel pins and, women, don't place the pin to attract attention to your bust.

▶ Make a full-length jewelry check for proportion and balance.

17. Neck

▶ Is your signature a unique necklace? Do you always wear pearls? A single gold or silver chain can be attractive. For men, a necklace can send a "new money" message.

▶ For work, don't wear a necklace ending at the bustline. Anything which calls attention to our sex does not work at work. The business environment is to be asexual.

▶ Consider color for your necklaces (check page 165).

▶ Ties and scarves bring the eye to your face and words. They also bring completeness and balance to your ensemble. Is a bow tie your signature?

▶ Consider your neck length when determining the collars/necklines that are most flattering to you. A short neck is not good in a turtleneck; a long neck is not good in a deep V-neckline. An open collar lengthens your neck and is more casual than a buttoned-up collar.

CHEST

▶ Two dimensions for you to remember we will review again. You learned them in Chapter 7:

$3^1/_2$ inches and $^1/_2$ inch

Give or take $^1/_4$ inch, these dimensions are always okay, always in style, always classic:

$3^1/_2$ inches   ▶ lapel width
           ▶ shirt collar
           ▶ man's tie width

<table>
<tr><td>$^1/_2$ inch</td><td>▸ of cuff should show below jacket sleeves</td></tr>
<tr><td></td><td>▸ of collar should extend above jacket collar</td></tr>
</table>

1. Jacket

- Lapels lie flat.
- No bubble at the back of the neck.
- Inside pockets comfortably placed.
- The jacket buttons easily. If you are busty, buttoning your jacket could emphasize your bust and therefore your sexuality. If you are not busty, you can wear the jacket buttoned. A closed jacket is more authoritative and formal than an open one.
- Back vent hangs perpendicularly.
- Shorter length jackets make shorter people look taller.
- Well made and *well* designed.
- No threads, rips, spots.
- Man-tailored is classic and works in corporations and financial institutions. More flexibility is available in other work situations.
- A sleeve on a long-sleeved jacket should at least hit the wrist bone.
- Made of 100 percent wool, cotton, silk, or blends of natural fibers that look that way. The new synthetics work well, as does some spandex, in your business casual styles.
- Cardigan sweaters or vests can substitute for jackets in some work environments.
- Wear your best color. Neutrals are best for versatility.

2. Shirt

- No gapping when buttoned.
- Long sleeves hit wrist wrinkles.
- French cuffs are more formal than button cuffs, but nice. (Your signature?) Cuff links with matching sides are better than ones with one up and one down side.
- Made of 100 percent natural fiber or look as if they are.
- Not too ruffly for work, but simple ruffles are OK.
- Classic styles are best for work.
- One of the first body parts to age is the upper arms. Long sleeves look more businesslike.
- Another body part that shows age early is the neck. You will want to consider the higher cut collars to cover up your neck as its skin loosens. If your neck is short, this won't be as attractive (but neither will you have as much neck to show).

▸ Collars on shirts buttoned to the neck need to fit well, especially when accompanied by a tie. For dress shirts, buy the correct neck size.

▸ The V-neckline is attractive on most of us. An unbuttoned first button on a collared blouse will read a V-neck. For business, the closed collar is more professional looking and more formal. Unbutton your collar after work or when you want to appear less formal and more approachable.

▸ A monogram (if you should want to wear one) is nice if subtle: color (white thread on pale blue shirt, no high-contrast thread and shirt) and style (simple, small initials). Monograms are placed on the cuff or over the heart.

▸ Wear a shirt in your best colors; high or low contrast with blazer or sweater.

▸ A row of high-quality buttons (bone, pearl, natural materials) can draw the eye vertically and add height.

▸ Pleats or design details will add interest.

▸ Solids or conservative patterns work best for business.

3. Pocket Handkerchief

▸ Take care that the care you take is not too obvious. A perfectly folded silk square is not as appealing as one that looks casually placed. These squares can be used several ways:

1. Pick the hanky up from the center and place this part out of the pocket (the four corners go inside the pocket).

2. Same as above but fold down the middle part and place it in the pocket with the four corners barely sticking out.

3. Placed in as a folded square, extending out $^1/_4$ inch.

▸ Women may want to use pieces of lace rather than a true silk or cotton hanky. Or what about going to the secondhand shops and finding old hankies with a history?

▸ If you use your pocket handkerchief, don't let your use show. (One for show. One for blow.) You want a very clean hanky peaking from your pocket. Carry a useable hanky in another pocket or in your briefcase for those days of need. It is so much better to blow on linen than into a tissue, both for your nose and for your image. Executives or classy persons do not carry the crumpled-up tissues in their fists or leave them on chairs when they get up.

- ▶ Is a pocket handkerchief your signature?
- ▶ Don't match your handkerchief exactly to your tie. Rather, pick up a color in your shirt, suit, or tie, or just use white.
- ▶ Matching the value of the handkerchief and the blazer is a nice, subtle look.

4. Tie/Scarf

- ▶ An authoritative look is a tie in your rich red coloration worn with a white shirt and a dark, matched suit. If you don't wear a tie, but still want to appear powerful at work, you will want to devise another method of bringing the eye to your brilliant words! Women might choose a simple necklace, brooch or pin at the closed neck to bring the eye up—Men might try a buttoned shirt to accomplish the same thing. Your neckline treatment, whether it is a scarf, tie, or necklace, should complement your face shape and size and balance your total look.
- ▶ The most professional-looking tie and scarf patterns are:

| REPP | FOULARD | SOLID | PLAID |

| ART | PAISLEY | POLKADOT | CLUB | THEME |

Professional tie and scarf patterns.

> ▶ Playful and arty ties have become appropriate in many business situations.
>
> ▶ Be cautious of ties bearing controversial messages.
>
> ▶ The fabric of choice for a tie or scarf is silk.
>
> ▶ Be creative—use a scarf as an ascot. An open blouse is more casual, so those of you with casual jobs can wear ascots effectively. Any scarf can be worn inside an unbuttoned collar, or outside a buttoned collar.
>
> ▶ Scarves are more "in" sometimes than others.
>
> ▶ Scarves work with all kinds of collars: mandarin, ruffle, spread, button-down, Peter Pan. They work with collars up or down and with the jewel neckline. Wearing your collar up can look contrived.
>
> ▶ Consider colors—wear colors that work best with your individual undertones. A good place to add color in the corporate world is with the tie or scarf—your red or burgundy will say "notice me," those colors will carry the eye quickly to your words and will call attention to you in a group. The best place for color in corporate America is at the neck.

5. Lapel Pins

> ▶ Pins say something about your occupation, your hobbies and your affiliations. Be careful of controversial labels.
>
> ▶ Is your lapel pin your signature? A friend has a Metropolitan Museum of Art frog pin that supposedly whispers wise things into her ear. It was her signature until a man interviewing her for a job commented after the interview, "I couldn't take my mind off your pin." What she wanted was for him to focus his mind on her mind, not be distracted by her pin. So she doesn't wear it now for business. If she were in sales and she wanted to be remembered for something unique, she might wear this frog constantly.
>
> ▶ A pin is usually worn on the left lapel so the name tag can be pinned to the right side. Placing the name tag on the right enables the name to be easily read as you shake hands.

WAIST

1. Belt

> ▶ Belts add a finishing touch that shows you care enough about yourself to attend to details. Even if you wear a jacket, you might wear a belt. Belts complete a look.

A V-shaped belt slims more than one that goes straight across
at the waist.

- If your waist is not an asset, don't use color or
  detail to bring the eye to your waist. Match your
  belt to your clothing, with perhaps the touch of a
  gold buckle being all that is noticed. Definitely
  don't wear a large, western buckle on a large
  waist. A V-shaped belt for women slims more
  than a belt that goes straight across. If you are
  long (low) waisted, match the belt (at least the
  darkness) to the skirt or slacks so as to cause the
  eye to include the waist band with your lower half.
  If you are short (high) waisted, match your belt to
  your shirt and you will add the width of the
  waistband to your top and lengthen your waist.
- Women—a white or pastel belt will not work well
  for work, but light bone or taupe will.
- Men—stick with natural leather colors (e.g.
  brown, tan, or black)—no white or blue!
- Leather is the most appropriate material for belts
  at work. A gold or silver buckle will hold up
  longer than a leather-covered one, and a shiny
  touch at the waist finishes a look.
- Have you tied a string tautly around your waist to
  see where it naturally wants to go? This indicates
  the location and size of your waist. Measure the
  length of the string to determine your waist
  measurement. Are you increasing clothing waist
  size along with an increasing body girth? We look
  much better in waist bands with an inch of
  comfort than in waistbands pulled tight. It's hard
  to admit we need a bigger size, but once we do
  and get appropriate-sized clothing, we look
  slimmer than we did trying to squeeze into sizes
  too small.

2. Braces	▶ Suspenders work well for men with a large stomach.
	▶ Are braces your signature?
	▶ Wear button-on braces, not clip on ones.

HANDS/HIPS/LEGS

1. Nails	▶ Well-groomed hands and nails are essential to a well-groomed look. Good grooming is equated with caring for ourselves. In our society, poor grooming shows a lack of self-esteem and energy. Tired blood rarely commands a promotion.
	▶ Trim, file, and clean nails regularly. On the job, nails can't be so long that they look like they would hinder your work. If you are in a profession where clients scrutinize your hands (such as accounting, architecture, or sales) you especially need immaculate nails . . . no weekend mechanics please!
	▶ If you want attention drawn to your hands, women should go with colored nails. If like most businesspersons, you want the eye carried to your face, you will wear a neutral or clear polish. Dark-colored chipped nail polish shouts "unkempt!" If you have nails that peel and break, you may want to consider wrapped or sculptured nails for a well-groomed look. Or better yet, check out the new products that actually keep your nails from peeling and breaking. To prevent your nails from yellowing, use a base coat with whichever color you choose. You may choose to wear no polish at all and buff your nails using a polishing cream. Buffing and manicures are healthy for men and women.
3. Pants	▶ $1^{1}/_{2}$ inches is the classic width for waist bands and pant cuffs.
	▶ Trousers can make us look tall, especially if we tie the color of our shoes, socks, pants, and top together—all close in value.
	▶ Good fit is essential in pants. Check that they hang straight from your buttocks, no gapping zipper in front (when possible, women, use back or side zippers), not too tight! The classic length for pants is touching toe/foot juncture in front and slanting slightly downward in the back. Determine the shoes you will be wearing with a particular pair of pants before hemming the pants. If heel heights vary on the shoes you intend to wear, then slacks would look too short with

some, too long with others, and just right only occasionally. Fashion dictates pant lengths just as it does skirt lengths. But remember, the classic length will always be OK. So you can hem those wonderful wool trousers at a classic length and wear them for years with the same heel height.

▶ Cuffed pants add a horizontal line breaking the movement of the eyes upward. So don't cuff if your legs are short, or if you want to look taller. Cuffs do allow pants to hang more precisely. Sometimes cuffs are "in."

▶ Width at the bottom of pants varies also with fashion. If your feet are extra large, you will want your slacks wider to detract from the length of your feet. Usually you look longer legged with narrower-bottomed pants. Keep in mind BALANCE—with hips, feet, shoulder detail, hat, and so on.

▶ If you find a good brand of pants that complements your build, stick with that brand. All designers use their own variations on the fitting model and probably your best brand is fitted on your type model.

▶ Lined pants will hold their shape and need less cleaning than unlined pants. Especially loosely woven fabric pants should be lined. Some fabrics will span the seasons: lightweight, 100 percent wool gabardine; raw silk; heavy chino or cotton twill.

▶ Jeans are only appropriate in the most casual of settings and don't work well for business except where culturally mandated: businessperson in Anchorage, attorney at Levi Strauss in San Francisco, or cowboy anywhere! The jeans that test best for business are those that have been fitted exactly, neatly custom tailored for you. Not everybody looks good in jeans, though most bodies end up in jeans quite often!

▶ New fabrics with a little stretch offer comfort without sacrificing the look.

▶ Be careful that the jeans you choose are age appropriate.

▶ Many American women's hips are large in proportion to their shoulders. If you don't want to call attention to your hips, don't wear bright or light-colored pants without a jacket for camouflage. If you are a stringbean, bright and light works well on your hips.

If your feet are extra large, you may want pants with extra width at the bottom.

4. Skirts

To discover your best skirt length, hold up a large scarf or piece of fabric and move it up and down. Observe your leg and body proportion.

- ▶ Jackets covering the derrière will look better than shorter lengths with most pants on most bodies.
- ▶ You can have fun with colored kneehigh and patterned socks. If they are bright, the eye will be carried to your ankle. For each outfit and occasion ask, "Do I want that?"
- ▶ Kneehigh trouser socks work best because no leg shows when you sit down.
- ▶ Under no circumstances let an underpant line show under slacks. Try out thongs, pantyhose, boxers—no distraction from the smooth line, please.
- ▶ The same underpant rule applies for skirts.
- ▶ Lengths vary with fashion, but some lengths will be better for your body. To discover this length, holdup a large square scarf or piece of fabric and, moving this fabric up and down, observe your leg with the different lengths. Also notice body proportion. A good length for many legs, and the classic length, is $1^1/_2$ inches below the knee (three fingers below your kneecap). If you want the least hassle with classic style clothing, choose a length and stick with it. It will always look good on you.
- ▶ Weather may also determine your skirt length. A miniskirt in the Arctic is not recommended.
- ▶ Let your body type dictate the skirt styles that are best suited for you. For a rounded tummy, gently gathered or externally pleated skirts work well.
- ▶ Pleats or tucks in skirts carry the eye upward. An asymmetrical treatment is more slimming than pleats or tucks all the way around. If pleats are stitched down at the top, be sure that the stitching doesn't emphasize a protruding tummy or derrière.
- ▶ Slitted skirts make a sexy statement—a hint of leg peeks occasionally from the skirt. Therefore, slitted skirts may not be appropriate for your workplace. Get the movement ease that slits offer in narrow skirts by inverted pleats or a larger hem diameter. Wrap skirts conceal while we stand, but when we sit it can be a quite a different matter. Be careful wearing wrap skirts to the office. Experiment with wrapping a wrap skirt backward.
- ▶ Prints are not as authoritative as solids, so for work avoid all but the smallest or most subtle prints.

▶ Lined skirts eliminate the need for slips.

▶ Do not let slips show—from under the hem or out the slits. Also, they should not bunch and look lumpy.

▶ Fabrics can be selected to fit your personality type (nubby tweeds for sporty Yangs), your occupation (silks for the executive moving up), your allergies (no wool next to your skin if it causes welts or rashes), or taste. These considerations apply to fabrics in all clothing items. Once again, let fabrics look natural even if they may not be.

Often shoes command a lot of attention from people who are uncomfortable looking into people's eyes.

FEET

1. Shoes

▶ Shoes are the punctuation to the clothing statement. They are more than an accessory. They must be correct.

▶ If your shoes are the first thing a person notices about you, you are probably wearing the wrong pair of shoes.

▶ Often shoes command a lot of attention from people who are uncomfortable looking into our eyes.

▶ Two-toned shoes don't test well for most offices (two-toned bone are better than navy and white).

▶ Neutrals are the most versatile colors.

▶ When you find a brand of shoe that fits your foot well, remember it and look for it again. Do you have such a brand now?

▶ Leather is great! Also consider stretchy materials for comfortable toes and cushioned soles for years of walking.

▶ Men are particularly conscious of well-polished, repaired shoes and judge others by the care they take of their shoes.

▶ For women at the office, closed toe and heel shoes give the most authority, open backs are second, and strappy or open shoes are the least authoritative (most feminine automatically equals least powerful).

▶ Although higher heels ($2^1/_2$–3 inches) are flattering on most legs, they can damage feet, legs, and hips in later life. Do you want to wear them every day?

▶ If you look too precarious walking in your high heels, you will not be viewed as able to do good work.

▶ If you need a toe-out for comfort, yet you need authority, get the smallest toe-hole you can find.

2. Socks

Do not wear sandals with toed or
heeled hose.

- ▶ Taupe, bone, natural, or camel shoes match your leg and work well with most colored skirts because the eye does not zero in on your feet.
- ▶ Wedges or low heels are more comfortable for most feet than are flats or high heels.
- ▶ We need to realize when we are young how important our feet are and treat them kindly: plenty of toe room, maybe orthotics, always good fit.
- ▶ Men—match your sock value to your shoes, your pants, or your tie if you dare. And let no hairy leg show when you sit.
- ▶ If your pants are a bit too short wear socks that match your slacks and shoes.
- ▶ If you buy several pairs of the same sock, two lost singles does not equal two lost pairs!
- ▶ Women—for the office, neutral-colored hose or hose matching the value of skirt and shoe work well. No attention is brought to the leg, therefore no sexuality is involved. Opaque tights make a lot of sense. They last forever, they cover leg imperfections, and they can be thrown in the washer. Sometimes they are in fashion.
- ▶ Hosiery, like skirt length, may be weather driven.
- ▶ Clear nail polish does wonders for those holes on the soles of your hose.
- ▶ If you buy all the same color and brand of pantyhose you can cut off the leg that runs and when you get two one-legged pairs of hose, wear them together as a "new pair." If they are control-top, your top will really be controlled with the double layer. If you value comfort, you won't like that!
- ▶ Sheer-finished hose snag less often than the rougher finishes.
- ▶ Many snags occur when pulling pantyhose on. Are your nails ragged?
- ▶ Rarely would you wear sandals with hose. If you do, NO toed or healed hose.

BACKVIEW

- ▶ Remember, people see the back of you almost as much as the front of you, although it's a side of yourself you rarely see!
- ▶ With a handheld mirror, do a final check in the full-length mirror before you leave: hair combed, collar in place, tags tucked in, shirt tucked in, belt

"on target," midriff covered, buttons buttoned and in the correct holes, zippers zipped and lying flat, underwear invisible? Make adjustments. You really won't get another chance at this one!

EVERYTHING ELSE

1. Fragrance
   - ▶ For the office, a clean smell works best. Perfumes are made to sexually attract and were invented as a "cover up." Your coworkers will wonder what you are up to if you come to work with cologne, especially if you don't normally wear it.
   - ▶ Fragrances intrude into others' space. Wear little or none.

2. Matching Versus Coordination
   - ▶ A safe combination is all solids or solids with one print; Mortimer Levitt says: two plains with one fancy. It takes practice to put "fancies" together successfully. The distinctness and the scale of the prints to be combined must be different enough to make them work together. It also helps if you repeat one or some of the colors in the prints to be combined. Matching is not easy. If you buy clothing made of differing fibers dyed in the same dye lot, they may not look like they match because of the reflective surface of the fabrics (e.g. raw silk and silk). Our memory for color is very short, so wear or take along the item to be matched or complemented when you shop, and check the match in differing light and in daylight.

3. Matching Suit Versus Sport Jacket
   - ▶ The matched suit is more formal, authoritative and powerful, while the sport jacket is more informal, casual, and approachable.
   - ▶ If the sport jacket is the same value as the pant or skirt, the eye will connect the two visually and will make you look taller than if one is dark and the other light.

4. Patterns for Work
   - ▶ Solids give more authority than do patterns.
   - ▶ Patterns that are best for work are small and repetitive, like those found in men's ties (foulards, dots, clubs), or if they appear to be solids, when you squint at them from a distance of 20 feet (subtle paisley, challis, pin stripes, tattersall).
   - ▶ Consider scale. For example, if you are large-boned, small prints will look out of proportion on you unless they read as a solid.

5. Coat
   - ▶ If you can have only one coat, make it a trench coat or single-breasted raincoat. It can work for work or play. And can be worn year round. But

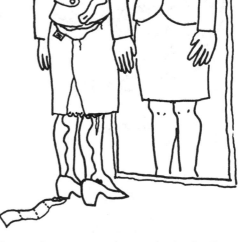

Remember . . . people see the back of you almost as much as the front of you, although it's a side of yourself you rarely see.

It takes practice to put "fancies" together successfully.

what do you do when it needs to be cleaned? It is better to have two coats for that reason, if for no other.

▸ Your full-length coats should be long enough to cover your longest skirt, or at least midcalf for men.

▸ Consider the best style and texture for your build, personality, taste, and lifestyle. For example, a classic single-breasted, navy Chesterfield for the corporate person who wants to look tall and lean and sophisticated; the tweedy gray-and-white short coat for the salt-and-pepper-haired college professor who wants to look sporty.

▸ Be careful wearing fur or leather coats to work. Think through the message you want to project.

6. Briefcase/ Purse

▸ A streamlined look is important. You don't want to look like you're burdened with everything but the kitchen sink.

▸ If you carry a briefcase, it is best not to also carry a purse. Women tend to carry everything, just in case. Decide what is necessary and plan places these items can be kept (desk drawer, glove box in car, small envelope purse inside briefcase, suit pockets).

▸ If you want to look career oriented, carry a briefcase even if you have nothing to carry in it but a magazine. A person with a briefcase means a businessperson. The more formal, authoritative briefcases are of dark stiff, nonexpandable suitcase-style leather with a handle and lock. Lighter-colored, soft, expandable leather, canvas, or nylon briefcases are more casual and would be more appropriate for counselors, artists, or noncorporate persons. Leather envelope-style briefcases are also an option.

7. Props

▸ Your artifacts are your object language. They make an important statement about you and a big impression on many people. They say something about your work, hobbies, and success. Carry quality props to look successful.

▸ Pen—gold, black, or silver ballpoints or fountain pens are classier than felt-tips, quantity-purchase plastic ballpoints, or the pen with the bank name printed on the side and the chain hanging off the top. . .

▸ Umbrella—black or other neutral collapsible style, men's style with a tortoise-shell handle, functional, not tattered or torn, perhaps one of your signatures—quality! Does it brighten your gloomy day?

- ▶ Wallet/Checkbook/Calendar/Coinpurse—leather or high-tech synthetic, quality look, not overstuffed, not torn.
- ▶ Calculator—looks expensive.
- ▶ Pill case—small, metal or "classy" plastic, without "aspirin" printed on the top.
- ▶ Key case—metal, leather, sterling, small or none (keys carry in pocket).
- ▶ Sunglasses—not too dark, expensive looking, to be taken off when talking to someone.
- ▶ Belts, briefcase, purses, calculators, palm pilots, laptop cases, jewelry, tape recorder are all considered props and need to look sufficiently rich.
- ▶ Cell phone and pager, the smaller, the better to be seen but not heard.
- ▶ Car, Office, Home, Memos—though not a part of dress, these are a big part of the total look. Think through these carefully, also. Make them match you. Use good taste and look successful.

Your professional image can be ruined if you pull out the wrong pen.

8. Dress

- ▶ Not as economical as separates but easy to slip into; ideally can be worn with jackets over, shirts underneath, and a variety of jewelry to expand usability.
- ▶ Classic style dresses (e.g. coatdresses or sheath) can be worn a lot of ways and can be made of fabrics that will work day or evening.

9. Underwear

- ▶ For work, invisible—no slips through slits, bra straps from blouses, BVD elastic above the belt line. If it's not designed to be seen, hide it!
- ▶ Should be comfortable; not constricting.
- ▶ Can be ruffly, romantic, feminine, or with a playful print under your power suit.

Go back to the "Total Look Exercise" on pages 190–195 and check in column two what you now think you want to improve. You may want to cover these two columns and have friends check off your "areas for improvement" in columns three through six.

What do you plan to do to transform your "areas for improvement" into the "ideal total look?" Complete the "Improvement Plan" in your journal.

● ●

Improvement plan

To Do	Date	Completed
_____	_____	_____
_____	_____	_____
_____	_____	_____
_____	_____	_____
_____	_____	_____
_____	_____	_____
_____	_____	_____
_____	_____	_____
_____	_____	_____
_____	_____	_____

● ●

Mark your calendar to come back in one month and mark column seven on pages 190–195. How have you improved?

Your total look is the sum of all parts. Once you have carefully considered and attended to each detail, you can be confident that your look is the best it can be. With practice, attending to all details will become second nature.

Then—on with life!

review

What do you remember about this chapter that is significant to *you*? First, list surprises, "ahas," lightbulbs in the page of your journal that follows. Then, look back through this chapter and list those discoveries you want to highlight.

● ● ● ● ● ● ● ● ● ● ● ● ● ● ● ● ● ● ● ●

Review: chapter 8

"Ahas"

1. _____

   _____

2. _____

   _____

3. _____

   _____

Discoveries to highlight

_____

_____

_____

_____

_____

_____

● ● ● ● ● ● ● ● ● ● ● ● ● ● ● ● ● ● ● ●

The review page at the end of this chapter will be useful later as you want to review *Dress Smart*. You won't need to reread the chapter, just your "ahas."

get organized

9

Wouldn't it be nice if you could stick your hand into your closet and everything you pulled out would be something you loved to wear? Again and again, everything you touched would be wonderful and would make you happy. It's possible and in fact, it's recommended! Remember that organization is not an end in itself, but a means to an end. It allows you to get on with the business of living. Let's get started.

The following are the steps we will examine:

1. Restructure the closet
2. Buy new hangers
3. Sort your clothing
4. Rehang the clothing you adore
5. Work with the so-so pile
6. Work with your recycle pile
7. Think about your wardrobe needs
8. List your wardrobe needs
9. Prioritize your wardrobe needs
10. Shop for your wardrobe needs

step 1: restructure the closet

Begin by studying your closet. Does it have the typical one rod topped by a single shelf? Maybe there is a hook or two? Or maybe you are lucky enough to have a couple of bars, several shelves, and lots of hooks. Think creatively about changes that can be made. Although we can't see your exact closet, we can say that almost every closet can benefit from:

▸ Double-hung rods that fit your shirts and skirts/pants
▸ A couple of shelves above the rods. Shelves above rods also serve as dust protectors.
▸ Shelves, hooks, and/or baskets covering every wall and the inside of the closet door.
▸ A good paint job.
▸ A light.

You can take measurements and buy materials and redo your closet yourself, you can hire a carpenter or handyperson to do it for you, or you can hire one of the many closet companies to make your closet as efficient as possible. This would be the ideal time, DRESS

Sketch some ideas for reorganizing your closet.

SMART-WISE, to redo your closet, but such a project may not fit in now with your budget or time commitments. Go ahead with this chapter even if *it is not time* for you to redo, but before you go ahead, make a commitment to yourself and your life to "efficientize" your closet at a certain time. Write it on your calendar and then continue planning and picturing this ideal structure. It is amazing what "a place for everything" will do for neatness, calmness, and decision-making. Keep your eyes open for pictures of closets you like and post them so they will inspire you. Keep your ears open for places to buy shelves and people to design your structure. Write these names in your journal for future use.

● ●

Closet redesign

Possible vendors

_____

_____

_____

Sketches

Using the graph pages, sketch some ideas for your closet. Measure and sketch again. You may want to get help from interior designers, closet consultants, or architects. Remember, if your closet is not ample you will not want to fill it with heavy wood dividers. A lighter wire-type organizational system would be more efficient. Think about placing everything you will wear together in your closet: sweaters, jewelry, belts, scarves. It is much easier to be able to *see* your accessories and clothing items as you choose your outfit each day than it is to try to *remember* what you have stored in various drawers and closets throughout the house. Opaque containers inside the closet don't work. You need to *see* to remember quickly what you have. And an organized closet is about dressing effectively and quickly.

If now *is the time* for your closet's update, begin working your plan. If you have no place other than the closet to hang things during the remodeling, remove everything from the closet only after you have all the materials together and are ready to construct. Do all painting, nailing, gluing, sawing, and hanging before you put anything back into your closet. And then put back only things you *wear* (no books or suitcases) and things you *love* (not just like). Is

that kind of scary? Are you afraid your closet will be empty if you put in only the clothes you love? Let's wait and see.

step 2: buy new hangers

Buy approximately 100 tubehangers and several skirt/slack hangers all in the same color. Buy the skirt/slack kind that stack several items vertically if horizontal space is at a premium. Buy enough wooden curved hangers for your blazers and suit jackets. These are the kinds of hangers suits come on when you buy them at good stores.

Sort your clothing.

step 3: sort your clothing

An easy way to sort is to place each item of clothing into one of three piles as you remove it from the closet:

1. Adore
2. So-so
3. Recycle

Put only clothes you love and wear in the "adore" pile. If you wear it, but have some ambivalent feelings about it, put it in the "so-so" pile. Move *quickly*. Don't analyze your pieces yet—let your instinct help you sort appropriately. The recycle pile will get those items that you will pass on to your sister, the local thrift shop, your friend who is your size and wears that color.

After your clothes, sort your shoes, scarves, jewelry, and all of your accessories. If you aren't going to remodel now, at least vacuum and dust while the closet is empty.

step 4: rehang the clothing you adore

Rehang your great clothing in the closet on your new hangers. Hang similar items together, facing in the same direction. Remove any belts and ties and pins and hang these with all the other belts and ties and pins. Separate any two-piece outfits and hang their parts with the appropriate items (e.g. its top with your blouses, its bottom with your skirts or slacks). You may not keep some outfits separated; but for now separating the items may surprise you by revealing exciting new combinations.

You have already thought a lot about what works for you and what you like. Put this information to use now. Figure out the things that make your great clothing great.

step 5: work with your "so-so" pile

This may be a really big job, requiring a lot of tough decisions. As you look at the item of clothing on top of this pile, ask yourself why it is so-so. Is it because it is:

- the wrong color
- too small or too large
- not your taste
- the wrong style for your body
- old, and you are tired of it
- ripped
- dirty
- scratchy
- not matching with anything else you own
- not made from a natural fiber
- outdated
- too "far out"
- poor quality
- out of season
- simply wrong, but you can't put your finger on why
- other reasons

In evaluation, ask yourself: Would I buy it today? Is it useful? Is it extremely beautiful? Does it have great sentimental value? If your so-so item meets none of these tests, it's probably not worth messing with.

If the *item is worth messing with* and if you are *willing to go to the trouble and the expense* to do what needs to be done to make it wearable, here are some suggestions:

A. Wrong Color
- Is it a natural fiber that can be dyed successfully? Synthetics don't take dye well.

- ▸ Can it be dyed to a darker color that will work better for you?
- ▸ Do you know a place that dyes clothing?
- ▸ Will you dye clothing?
- ▸ Will it likely shrink in the hot water dyes that we can buy?
- ▸ Do you know where to get cold water dyes?
- ▸ Do you know what color it will become once you add the dye to its present coloration?

B. Too Small or Too Large
- ▸ If it is too small, is there enough seam allowance to be let out?
- ▸ If it is let out, will the old seam lines show?
- ▸ If it did fit, would something else be wrong with it, and you wouldn't wear it anyway?
- ▸ Could you do the work yourself?
- ▸ Do you know a good seamstress or tailor who could do the work?
- ▸ Is the garment worth the expense involved?
- ▸ Do you like the fabric well enough to have another garment made of it?
- ▸ Can the gapping button-down-the-front shirt be carefully sewn up and pulled on over the head?
- ▸ Can you let out the waist and wear braces (suspenders) to keep the pants at your midriff? Be sure to buy the button-on braces, not the clip-on type.

C. Not Your Taste
- ▸ Does it look like your best friend and could you give it to that person? (Or did they give it to you?)
- ▸ Could you change a feature and make it your taste (e.g. change the pleat direction or buttons)?

D. Wrong Style for Your Body
- ▸ Could you make it right for your body: shorten jacket if you are short, change collar from round to V if you have a round face.

E. Old
- ▸ Is there a way to revive it, make it seem young again?

F. Ripped
- ▸ Can it be successfully repaired?
- ▸ Can you do it, or do you know someone who can?

G. Dirty
- ▸ Can it be cleaned?
- ▸ If there is a spot, will it come out? If not, can you cover it with something? Patch? Pin? Monogram?
- ▸ Have you checked with an extension agent about removing those spots that remain after several cleanings?

Can the gapping button-down-the-front shirt be sewn up and pulled on over the head?

Can it be updated (lapels narrowed, flap or trim removed, pants pegged?) Or will fashion catch up with it?

H. Scratchy
- ▶ Can a tag be cut out or a lining added to keep it from bothering you?
- ▶ Could you wear some article of clothing underneath?

I. Nothing to Go with It
- ▶ Do you like it well enough to buy items to go with it?
- ▶ Do you need another person's eye to show you that actually you do have some things to go with it?

J. Not Natural Fibers
- ▶ Are you really particular now and refuse to wear synthetics? Or even blends?

K. Outdated
- ▶ Can it be updated: lapels narrowed, flaps or trim removed, skirt or slacks shortened or lengthened, pants pegged.
- ▶ Is it a dated fabric that is impossible to help? Is it old, but not yet vintage?

L. Far Out
- ▶ If it is dramatic and you don't like to stand out, could it be "dedramatized?"
- ▶ If it is high fashion and you like classic things, could you make it more classic?

M. Poor Quality
- ▶ Probably nothing can be done if this is the case. Live and learn.

N. Out of Season
- ▶ Is it short sleeved and you only wear long-sleeved shirts under your suits?
- ▶ Is it too light a color for winter?

O. Simply Wrong. But You Can't Put Your Finger on Why.
- ▶ You may be intuitively tuning in to imperil . . . baggage attached to that item: the item was manufactured without love; bad associations (e.g. wore it to your mother's funeral, or to dinner and lifeboating on the *Titanic*). There is no remedy. Toss this item.
- ▶ The wrong mood for the place (e.g. it was great in Honolulu, but its not happy in Hoboken). Do you want to save it for a trip back to Hawaii?

P. Other Reasons
- ▶ Can you think of remedies?

If the garment *is not worth it,* and if you would *rather buy a new one* than mess with what it would take to make it right, put it in the recycle pile. Remember, sometimes one part of an outfit is "save" and another part is "recycle."

If you can't part with the item, yet you are not wearing it, hang it in another closet, your "stand-by" area. DO NOT HANG SO-SO ITEMS IN WITH THOSE YOU ADORE. Remember, your aim is to have in your closet only those items you adore, those that make you happy and that make you feel wonderful. These clothes in your "stand-by" area will be available to wear when necessary, when missed, when you have lost those ten pounds. Periodically you can check this "stand-by" area to see if you have missed any of the items. If you haven't and if a year—or two or three—go by, and you have not missed them (and you are not holding on to them for sentimental reasons), you should seriously consider recycling them.

If the garment *is worth it* and *you are willing* to expend the energy, then place this item in the appropriate pile for transformation:

1. Dye
2. Alter and mend yourself
3. Alter and mend by tailor
4. Send to cleaners
5. Wash

Follow the preceding procedure for all of your "so-so" clothes and accessories.

Hopefully your items in the piles for transformation will be transformed from "so-so" to "adore." The problem that may occur with some is that you may have misdiagnosed their ailments when you originally analyzed them. For example, your skirt hung crookedly with side seams off and was poorly made, and it didn't fit. Now that it fits, it is still of poor quality. It fits, and it is still so-so. Now you can recycle it.

Establish the habit of hanging only clothing in your closet that is wearable. If it has a spot, get the spot out immediately. The longer any spot remains, the harder it is to remove. If an item is torn, put it in with your mending (out of your closet). When it is repaired, hang it back in your closet.

step 6: work with your recycle pile

This pile is much *easier* to handle than your so-so pile. You may just want to put all these items in a garbage bag and get them out of your sight before you change your mind and start questioning your decision. You may want to sort this pile into those clothes to:

- ▶ give to a friend
- ▶ give to a relative
- ▶ put in the dress-up trunk
- ▶ sell on consignment (these items need to be in good shape, have no holes, be clean, and in style)
- ▶ give to Goodwill or a homeless shelter or some not-for-profit agency for tax credit (look in the phone book and call to see if they pick up)

It is amazing how freeing it is to get rid of unneeded things, clothing included. You will feel lighter and almost cleansed when these unworn clothes are gone. And you become open and receptive to those new clothing items that you will "adore." So get rid of them soon.

step 7: think about your wardrobe needs

As you examine the closet full of the clothes you "adore," think creatively. Now that you have hung that suit as separates, do you see the skirt or pants working with another of your jackets? Hold up each bottom (skirt, slacks, shorts, culottes) next to each top (jacket, sweater, shirt, vest). Do they go together? You may want a friend or a wardrobe consultant to help you figure out new ways to combine your present "adorable" wardrobe. Ask yourself, "where are the gaps?" If you just had a charcoal pant could you have two new business looks? You may be able to look at your closet and see where you are lacking (e.g. do you have five pair of slacks and ten jackets?).

What is missing may not become obvious until you complete the closet inventory in your journal. Look at the clothes you "adore" and list each item in the chart below.

● ● ● ● ● ● ● ● ● ● ● ● ● ● ● ● ● ● ●

_____'s Closet Inventory Date: _____

Suits

Fall/Winter   Year Round   Spring/Summer
_____
_____
_____
_____
_____
_____
_____
_____
_____
_____
_____
_____
_____

Vests

Fall/Winter   Year Round   Spring/Summer
_____
_____
_____
_____
_____
_____
_____
_____
_____
_____
_____
_____

_____

_____

Jackets

Fall/Winter	Year Round	Spring/Summer

_____

_____

_____

_____

_____

_____

_____

_____

_____

_____

_____

_____

_____

_____

Skirts

Fall/Winter	Year Round	Spring/Summer

_____

_____

_____

_____

_____

_____

_____

_____

_____

_____

_____

_____

_____

_____

Pants

Fall/Winter	Year Round	Spring/Summer

_____

_____

_____

_____

_____

_____

_____

_____

_____

_____

_____

_____

_____

Shirts

Fall/Winter	Year Round	Spring/Summer

_____

_____

_____

_____

_____

_____

_____

_____

_____

_____

_____

_____

_____

_____

_____

_____

Sweaters

Fall/Winter	Year Round	Spring/Summer

_____

_____

Dresses

Fall/Winter   Year Round   Spring/Summer
_____

_____

_____

_____

_____

_____

_____

_____

_____

_____

_____

_____

_____

_____

Shoes

Fall/Winter   Year Round   Spring/Summer
_____

_____

_____

_____

_____

_____

_____

_____

_____

_____

_____

_____

_____

_____

_____

Hose and Socks

Fall/Winter	Year Round	Spring/Summer

Belts

Fall/Winter	Year Round	Spring/Summer

_____
_____
_____
_____
_____
_____
_____
_____
_____
_____
_____
_____
_____

Purses/Briefcases

Fall/Winter	Year Round	Spring/Summer

_____

_____

Scarves/Ties

Fall/Winter   Year Round   Spring/Summer
_____

_____

_____

_____

_____

_____

_____

_____

_____

_____

_____

_____

_____

_____

Jewelry

Fall/Winter   Year Round   Spring/Summer
_____

_____

_____

_____

_____

_____

_____

_____

_____

_____

_____

_____

_____

_____

_____

Coats

Fall/Winter	Year Round	Spring/Summer

_____

_____

_____

_____

_____

_____

_____

_____

_____

_____

_____

_____

_____

_____

_____

_____

Hats

Fall/Winter	Year Round	Spring/Summer

_____

_____

_____

_____

_____

_____

_____

_____

_____

_____

_____

_____

_____

Gloves

Fall/Winter	Year Round	Spring/Summer

_____

_____

_____

_____

_____

_____

_____

_____

_____

_____

_____

_____

Now go back to the beginning of your inventory and check those items that represent your major lifestyle wardrobe category (e.g. career, casual, sport, business casual). Determine if your current wardrobe matches your lifestyle needs? Do you see any glaring holes? List the clothing that will plug those holes on the wardrobe needs chart.

step 8: list your wardrobe needs

● ● ● ● ● ● ● ● ● ● ● ● ● ● ● ● ● ● ●

Wardrobe needs

Clothing item	Description	Fabric	Color	Season

step 9: prioritize your wardrobe needs

Number each item listed on your wardrobe needs chart. When you go shopping, look for the most important items first.

step 10: shop for your wardrobe needs

But you have no money to spend on your wardrobe, you say? This shopping step may have to wait, and if it does, you can do some thinking in the interim about how you can buy yourself the clothing that will:

▶ fill your wardrobe gaps
▶ fit your body,
   personality,
   style,
   values, and
   pocketbook
▶ make you feel authentic and wonderfully "you"

Remember that *you* are worth the money it takes to make you look and feel terrific.

Just as you budget for food or rent, budget a given amount for clothing. Then when you see a special item that will make your wardrobe and your heart sing, you will have no guilt about buying it since the money is already allocated.

Think creatively! One of our friends slips every stray $20 bill into an envelope and uses the accumulation to buy wearable art.

Change your point of view. Think of your clothing as *investments* rather than *expenses*! Buy quality, classic clothing that will last for years. Focus on cost-per-wear; amortize your clothing over the time you will be wearing it.

Remember, you can *accumulate* good clothing over the years. You don't have to go out right now and buy it all. Be patient. Build up a reservoir of wonderful clothing pieces that are just right for you.

You may need some of the clothing now (e.g. the suits if you are interviewing for jobs). You might want to borrow money to buy the

We'll get back to you.

interview clothes that will get you the job (because they will make you look and feel confident and competent), which will get you the money to pay back the loan. Too many people think about this backwards. They wait to get the job to get the money to get the professional clothing which could have gotten them the job much more quickly and easily. It may be much more difficult for them to get a job because of how they feel and look when they go on interviews. Remember that four minutes after the interview starts, it may be all over. Your clothing can make the difference between "when can you start" and "we'll get back to you." Don't let the way you look be a detriment. *Get in the door* and show them how competent you are.

In Chapter 10, we will deal with the wise ways to acquire those needed wardrobe components.

review

What do you remember about this chapter that is significant to *you*? First, list surprises, "ahas," lightbulbs in the page of your journal that follows. Then, look back through this chapter and list those discoveries you want to highlight.

● ●

Review: chapter 9

"Ahas"

1. _____

   _____

2. _____

   _____

3. _____

   _____

Discoveries to highlight

_____

_____

_____

_____

_____

_____

● ●

The review page at the end of this chapter will be useful later as you want to review *Dress Smart*. You won't need to reread the chapter, just your "ahas."

acquire components

If you have gotten this far in *Dress Smart*, you are well on your way to shopping wisely and well. Today you will make fewer mistakes in acquiring your clothing components than ever before.

There are a number of reasons why people are either happy or unhappy with their clothing. If you become conscious of the reasons that are important to you, you can consistently purchase clothing that satisfies you. What do you value in your clothing?

clothing value

analyze your clothing values

The following information is based on research by Anna Creekmore. It was developed into the "Clothing Value Analysis" by clothing designer and artist, Mary Byington.

To determine what you value in your clothing, turn to questions 13 to 15 in the questionnaires in Chapter 1 (women) and questions 21 to 23 in Chapter 2 (men). Add up the numbers. Then, check the boxes in the "Clothing values" chart that match your answers and total the number for each letter. The lowest sums indicate those values which are most important to you. The highest sums are your least important values.

● ● ● ● ● ● ● ● ● ● ● ● ● ● ● ● ● ● ● ●

Clothing values

Women

13a___	13b___	13c___	13d___	13e___	13f___	13g___
14a___	14b___	14c___	14d___	14e___	14f___	14g___
15a___	15b___	15c___	15d___	15e___	15f___	15g___
Total	Total	Total	Total	Total	Total	Total

Men

21a___	21b___	21c___	21d___	21e___	21f___	21g___
22a___	22b___	22c___	22d___	22e___	22f___	22g___
23a___	23b___	23c___	23d___	23e___	23f___	23g___
Total	Total	Total	Total	Total	Total	Total

Analysis

1. For which letter did you get the lowest sum? _____

2. For which letter did you get the highest sum? _____

3. Were you approximately equal on several letters? _____

4. Which ones were lowest? _____

● ● ● ● ● ● ● ● ● ● ● ● ● ● ● ● ● ● ● ●

interpret your clothing values

Check the values below that correspond to your lowest and highest letters. Read the description of these values.

A—*ECONOMIC:* The amount of money and time spent on clothing is important. You may want fewer items of clothing, or you may be willing to spend more time and money if you are assured that the result will be a good investment.

B—*THEORETICAL:* You like clothes that tell a story or express an idea. Ordinary, store-bought items will be boring to you.

C—*COMFORT:* Physical comfort tends to be more important than style, color, price, or other such factors. Your attention is best directed toward finding socially acceptable, comfortable clothing.

D—*AESTHETIC:* You prefer beautiful clothes. Your definition of beautiful may be different from that of others; the aesthetic can indicate a degree of individuality. Top quality is essential.

E—*BODY AWARENFSS:* Your preference is for clothing that enhances your body. You will want to dress to enhance your body's best features. If your body could be improved through diet, exercise, or both, you will want to make that effort, for only then will you be satisfied.

F—*SOCIAL:* Satisfying a preference for clothing that is socially acceptable is simple because you can follow the newest fashions or prescribed career apparel. Be sure to buy moderately styled clothing that you intend to wear for several seasons. Spend less money on clothing that you intend to wear one or two seasons only.

G—*POLITICAL:* It is important for you to be the "best-dressed" person in a situation. You need to be willing to spend more time and money on clothing than average.

summarize your values

Are you surprised by your responses? This value knowledge can help you make wise buying decisions. If you are high comfort, for example, and you find a wonderful pair of pants on sale that are a bit snug right now, but you know you will love wearing them once you lose those ten pounds, don't buy them. They will hang in your closet unworn because they are uncomfortable. And the most expensive clothes are those we don't wear. Let's repeat that: *THE MOST EXPENSIVE CLOTHES ARE THOSE WE DON'T WEAR.*

Your most expensive clothes are those you don't wear.

take buying action

If your body awareness value is important, you will want to exercise regularly. If aesthetic considerations are high, you will want to stop shopping at the "Cheap Shop." If you value economic considerations, you need to watch the way the clothing mixes back and forth. You will want to spend your important money on clothes you adore and wear.

If your list of wardrobe needs is long (see page 239) and if you are having a hard time rationalizing or even locating the amount of cash that will be required to purchase those items, you have several options. Before we get to these options however, please remember:

1. You must believe your clothing investment will be worthwhile.
2. You are wonderful, and you must let your clothing speak highly of you!
3. You are worth the best.

The options:

1. Borrow money
2. Sew
3. Wait for sales
4. Find discount or used clothing stores that carry quality clothing.

Whatever you do, *buy quality*, and be certain that your clothing mixes back and forth and that you purchase only items you adore.

Now, women look at Chapter 1, questions 72 to 78, and men look at Chapter 2, questions 75 to 81. Use this information to figure out some ways to further reduce your buying mistakes.

● ● ● ● ● ● ● ● ● ● ● ● ● ● ● ● ● ● ● ●

Buying guidelines

To Buy/Wear   *To Avoid*

Fabrics

I. _____   I. _____

2. _____   2. _____

3. _____   3. _____

4. _____   4. _____

5. _____   5. _____
6. _____   6. _____

7. _____   7. _____
8. _____   8. _____

Jewelry

I. _____   I. _____

2. _____   2. _____

3. _____   3. _____

4. _____   4. _____

5. _____   5. _____

Shoes

I. _____   I. _____

2. _____   2. _____

3. _____   3. _____

4. _____   4. _____

5. _____   5. _____

6. _____   6. _____

7. _____   7. _____

8. _____   8. _____

Purses/Briefcases

1. _____   1. _____

2. _____   2. _____

3. _____   3. _____

Underwear

1. _____   1. _____

2. _____   2. _____

3. _____   3. _____

Ties/Scarves

1. _____   1. _____

2. _____   2. _____

3. _____   3. _____

● ●

Now women look at questions 93 to 98; men look at questions 95 to 100.

To Buy/Wear   *To Avoid*

To Work Or to an Important Meeting

1. _____   1. _____

2. _____   2. _____

3. _____   3. _____

Around the House

1. _____   1. _____

2. _____   2. _____

3. _____   3. _____

To School

1. _____   1. _____

2. _____   2. _____

3. _____   3. _____

To Entertain

1. _____   1. _____

2. _____   2. _____

3. _____   3. _____

To Parties

1. _____   1. _____

2. _____   2. _____

3. _____   3. _____

To Exercise

1. _____   1. _____

2. _____   2. _____

3. _____   3. _____

Other Situations

1. _____   1. _____

2. _____   2. _____

3. _____   3. _____

● ● ● ● ● ● ● ● ● ● ● ● ● ● ● ● ● ● ● ●

present roles in life

Now women look at questions 81 and 82; men look at questions 84 and 85. Check your closet inventory in Chapter 9 to complete the following chart.

● ● ● ● ● ● ● ● ● ● ● ● ● ● ● ● ● ● ● ●

Present roles

1. Most time consuming role   1. Number of clothing items

   _____   you have which work for that

                                    role _____

Are your clothing quantities unbalanced for your present roles?

2. Least time consuming role   2. Number of clothing items you

_____   have which work for this role

                                    _____

3. Do you have too few clothes for the role in which you spend

   most of your time? _____

4. Are your clothing quantities unbalanced for your present roles?

   _____

5. How about in five years? _____

6. Should you accumulate more professional clothing because you

   will be working full time rather than part time?

7. If you are retiring, you can start looking for those superb

   leisure clothes.

● ●

Look at question 84 (women); question 87 (men). Determine if there is *any place* you spend a lot of time where you have an inadequate number of clothing items? For instance, if you are in your car most of the time, would you like to have a pair of driving shoes that you leave in the car and switch into to save wear and tear on your heels?

How about the next question? Do you have enough clothes for each role?

Women, consider question 77. Do you want to allow a large portion of your budget for fancy undies? If not, are you certain that you have allowed for the necessities, such as:

▶ half slip with a slit
▶ dark underwear/bra
▶ light underwear/bra
▶ racer back and/or strapless bra
▶ long slip if you have a long skirt
▶ camisole or full slip for translucent blouses
▶ underpants with no panty line

create a shopping plan

With a plan, you need not spend a lot of time shopping. You can probably shop twice a year, once in the fall and once in the spring, and buy most of your necessary clothing then. If you love to shop, you now can spend more time looking for your correct items.

Studies show that women with jobs are the worst impulsive buyers. It is usually better to think about an item before you buy, then to buy consciously. Your work on *Dress Smart* will help the impulse buys you *do* make work out better than average.

If you think through each of the following considerations each time you shop, you will shop more effectively and efficiently. Make some notes now about each item.

● ● ● ● ● ● ● ● ● ● ● ● ● ● ● ● ● ● ●

Shopping plan

Answer the following questions before you go on your next shopping trip.

1.   When do you shop? (Question 83 for women; question 86 for

     men.) Do you like your answer to this one? If not, what can

     you do to change?

_____

_____

2.   Think about the success stories in your closet. What is it

     about them that makes them do marvelous things for you?

---

3. Limit your colors to two or three basics and the accent colors
    that go with them. What are these colors?

    _____

    _____

    _____

4. What do you value most in your clothes: aesthetics, economy,
    comfort, body awareness, or social, political, or theoretical
    considerations?

    _____

5. If economic considerations are important, be aware of sales:
    after Easter, after July 4th, after Christmas. When will you shop?

    _____

6. If you have difficulty finding clothes, shop early in the season:
    in August for fall and winter; in March for spring and
    summer. When will you shop?

    _____

7. If you are interested in being up to date with fashion,
    research fashion magazines and ads for current styles.
    Observe the way people you admire dress. Attend fashion
    shows. Have you done these things? _____ When will you?

    _____

8. You made a shopping list and prioritized the items on your
    list. Are there any changes you want to make now?

    _____

    _____

    _____

    _____

9. Determine your shopping budget. What is it for this trip?

   _____

10. Know your stores. Are there others you will go to besides
    those listed in question 111 for women and question 113 for
    men?

    _____

    _____

    _____

● ●

final checklist

Plan to dress well when you shop and wear clothing that is easy to
slip on and off. When you see an item on your list, buy it then.
Don't procrastinate. But, if you have a question about an item, do
not buy it then. Sleep on your decision or buy it knowing you may
have to return it.

Buy the best quality you can afford. Consider the cost-per-wear.
Read the label and think about the care involved.
Choose good natural fibers or quality synthetics.
Buy solids before plaids or patterns.
Only buy a dress if the look can be changed with jackets, belts,
and other accessories.

Spend the largest portion of your money on the clothes you wear
most often—and especially clothes for your upper half (jackets,
blouses, scarves/ties). These are the clothes that are seen more over
the desk top or the dinner table. These clothes are near your face,
which is where the eye spends most of its time.
Look at the store's displays for ideas on accessories.
Ask yourself about each clothing item you are considering:

► Do I feel comfortable in it physically and psychologically?
► Does it suit my "personal style?"
► Is it a classic style, or does it need to be?
► If the fit or proportion is wrong, am I willing to pay for alter-
  ations?

Spend most of your money on the upper half; the clothes seen
over desktops.

▶ Can it do double duty?
▶ Will it pull together several items in my wardrobe to open new
  options?
▶ Does it go with at least three other pieces in my wardrobe?
▶ Does the mood match the mood of the items I want to wear it
  with?
▶ Can I wear it without spending a lot on accessories?
▶ Is the color wonderful on me?
▶ Does the fabric cross three seasons?
▶ Do I look like the person I want to be?
▶ Does it help me project the image I desire?
▶ Does it look *great* on me?

Unless you love to shop, searching for clothes can be a real pain.
With your mind loaded with your newly acquired knowledge, this
wardrobe acquisition process has been made easier. You have a plan.
You have thought through what is important to you, and you know
what you want and need. Now when you are ready to acquire your
wardrobe components, chances are you'll have fun!

review

What do you remember about this chapter that is significant to *you*? First, list surprises, "ahas," lightbulbs in the page of your journal that follows. Then, look back through this chapter and list those discoveries you want to highlight.

● ● ● ● ● ● ● ● ● ● ● ● ● ● ● ● ● ● ● ●

Review: chapter 10

"Ahas"

1. _____

   _____

2. _____

   _____

3. _____

   _____

Discoveries to highlight

_____

_____

_____

_____

_____

_____

● ● ● ● ● ● ● ● ● ● ● ● ● ● ● ● ● ● ● ●

The review page at the end of this chapter will be useful later as you want to review *Dress Smart*. You won't need to reread the chapter, just your "ahas."

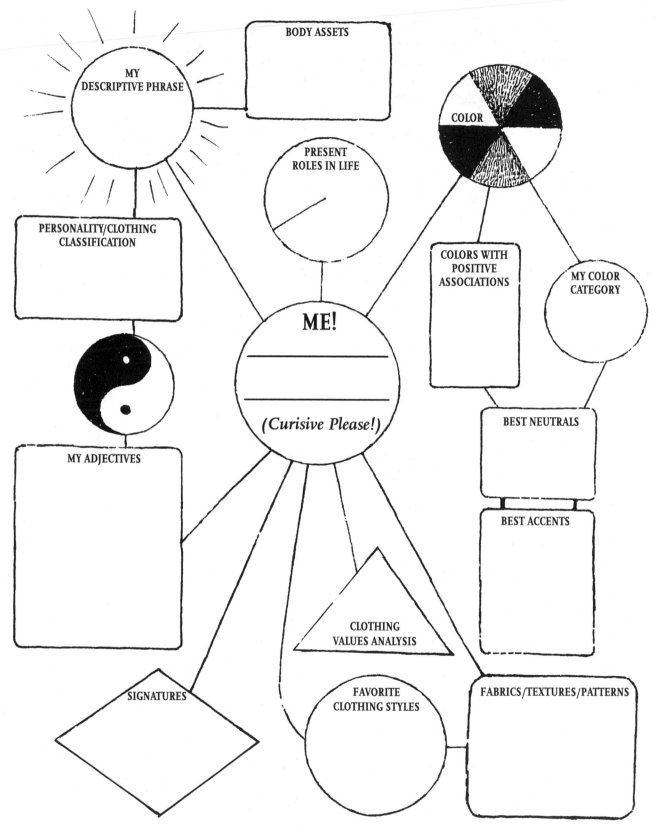

My map to personal authenticity.

image/wardrobe bibliography

men

Flusser, Alan. *Making the Man: The Insider's Guide to Buying & Wearing Men's Clothes*. New York: Simon & Schuster, 1981.

Furstenberg, Egon von. *The Power Look*. New York: Holt, Rinehart & Winston Co., 1978.

Gross, Kim Johnson, Jeff Stone, and Kristina Zimbalist. *Chic Simple Dress Smart for Men: Wardrobes That Win in the New Workplace*. New York: Warner, 2002.

Hix, Charles, and Brian Burden. *Dressing Right*. New York: St. Martin's Press, 1978.

Jackson, Carole, and Kalia Lulow. *Color for Men*. New York: Ballantine Books, 1984.

Levitt, Mortimer. *The Executive Look: How to Get It, How to Keep It*. New York: Atheneum Publishers, 1982.

Marquand, Ed. *Beyond Soap, Water, & Comb: A Man's Guide to Good Grooming and Fitness*. New York: Abbeville Press, 1998.

McGill, Leonard. *Stylewise: A Man's Guide to Looking Good for Less*. New York: G.P. Putnam's Sons, 1983.

Molloy, John T. *Dress for Success*. New York: Warner Books, Inc., 1978.

Naifeh, Steven Woodward, and Gregory White Smith. *Moving Up in Style: The Successful Man's Guide to Impeccable Taste*. New York: St. Martin's Press, 1980.

Thompson, Jacqueline. *Image Impact for Men: The Business and Professional Man's Personal Packaging Program*. New York: Dodd, Mead and Company, 1983.

Thourlby, William. *You Are What You Wear: The Key to Business Success*. New York: NAL, 1980.

women

Arpel, Adrien, and Ronnie S. Ebenstein. *How to Look 10 Years Younger*. New York: Rawson, Wade Publishers, Inc., 1980; New York: Warner Books, Inc., 1981.

Audette, Vicki. *Dress Better for Less*. Deephaven, MN: Meadowbrook Press, Inc., 1981.

August, Bonnie. *Looking Thin: The Famous Designer's Guide to Reshaping Your Body and Concealing Almost Any Figure Flaw with Clothes*. New York: Rawson Associates, 1981.

Bandy, Way. *Designing Your Face*. New York: Random House, Inc., 1984.

The Beauty Experts at Mary Kay Cosmetics. *The Mary Kay Guide to Beauty: Discovering Your Special Look*. Reading, MA: Addison-Wesley Publishing Co., 1983.

Berenson, Marisa. *Dressing Up: How to Look and Feel Absolutely Perfect for Any Social Occasion*. New York: G.P. Putnam's Sons, 1984.

Berg, Rona. *Beauty: The New Basics*. New York: Workman Publishing, 2001.

Binder, Pearl. *Dressing Up, Dressing Down*. Winchester, MA: Unwin, Inc., 1986.

Calasibetta, Charlotte, and Hyman Mankey. *Essential Terms of Fashion: A Collection of Definitions*. New York: Fairchild Publications, 1986.

Cass, Lee Hogan, and Karen E. Anderson. *Look Like a Winner: Why, When, and Where to Wear What*. New York: G.P. Putnam's Sons, 1985.

Cho, Emily. *Looking, Working, Living Terrific 24 Hours a Day*. New York: G.P. Putnam's Sons, 1984.

Cho, Emily, and Hermine Lueders. *It's You: Looking Terrific Whatever Your Type*. New York: Ballantine Books, 1987.

Cho, Emily, and Linda Grover. *Looking Terrific: Express Yourself Through the Language of Clothing*. New York: G.P. Putnam's Sons, 1978; New York: Ballantine Books, 1979.

Coffey, Barbara. *Glamour's Success Book*. New York: Simon & Schuster, Inc., 1979.

Constantine, Susannah, and Trinny Woodall. *What Not to Wear*, Orion Publishing Company, 2002.

Constantine, Susannah, and Trinny Woodall. *What Not to Wear, Part 2: For Every Occasion*. Weidenfeld Nicolson Illustrated, 2003.

Craighead, Joni. *First Impressions: Tips to Enhance Your Image*. Omaha, NE: Addicus Books, 1996.

Dano, Linda, with Anne Kyle. *Looking Great . . . It Doesn't Have to Hurt*. New York: The Berkeley Publishing Group, 1997.

Delong, Marilyn Revell. *The Way We Look: Dress and Aesthetics*, 2nd Edition. New York: Fairchild Publications, 1998.

Fatt, Amelia. *Conservative Chic: The 5-Step Program for Dressing With Style*. New York: Times Books, 1983.

Feldon, Leah. *Does This Make Me Look Fat?* New York: Villard, 2000.

Feldon, Leah. *Dressing Rich*. New York: G.P. Putnam's Sons, 1982.

Fendel, Alyson. *Waiting in Style: A Maternity Wardrobe That Works*. Washington, DC: Acropolis Books Ltd., 1983.

Fiedorek, Mary B., and Diana Lewis Jewell. *Executive Style: Looking It . . . Living It*. Piscataway, NJ: New Century Publishers, Inc., 1983.

Goday, Dale, with Molly Cochran. *Dressing Thin: How to Look Ten, Twenty, up to Thirty-Five Pounds Thinner Without Losing an Ounce!* New York: Simon & Schuster/Fireside, 1980.

Gross, Kim Johnson, Jeff Stone, and Rachel Urquhart. *Women's Wardrobe*. New York: Alfred A. Knopf, 1995.

Gross, Kim Johnson, Jeff Stone, and Kristina Zimbalist. *Chic Simple Dress Smart for Women: Wardrobes That Win in the Workplace*. New York: Warner, 2002.

Halbreich, Betty, with Sally Wadyka. *Secrets of a Fashion Therapist.* New York: Harper Collins, 1997.

Hensler, Tracy, and Carla Dougherty. *Sleek Chic: Head-to-Toe Fashion Strategies for Fixing Figure Flaws.* New York: G.P. Putnam's Sons, 1988.

Irons, Diane. *The Worlds Best-Kept Beauty Secrets: What Really Works in Beauty, Diet, & Fashion.* Naperville, IL: Sourcebooks, Inc., 1997.

Jackson, Carole. *Color Me Beautiful: Discover Your Natural Beauty Through the Colors That Make You Look Great and Feel Fabulous.* Washington, DC: Acropolis, 1980.

Johnson, Anna. *Three Black Shirts: All You Need to Survive.* New York: Workman Publishers, 2000.

Kinsel, Brenda. *In the Dressing Room with Brenda.* Berkeley, CA: Wildcat Canyon Press, 2001.

Kinsel, Brenda. *40 over 40: 40 Things Every Woman over 40 Needs to Know About Getting Dressed.* Berkeley, CA: Wildcat Canyon Press, 1999.

Klein, M.D., W. Arnold, James H. Sternberg, M.D., and Paul Bernstein. *The Skin Book: Looking and Feeling Your Best Through Proper Skin Care.* New York: Collier Books, 1980.

Klensch, Elsa, with Beryl Meyer. *Style.* New York: Berkeley Publishing Group, 1995.

Leopold, Allison Kyle, and Anne Marie Cloutier. *Short Chic.* New York: Rawson Wade Publishers, Inc., 1981.

Levene, Malcolm, and Kate Mayfield. *10 Steps to Fashion Freedom.* New York: Crown Publishers, 2001.

Mathis, Carla Mason, and Helen Villa Connor. *The Triumph of Individual Style: A Guide to Dressing Your Body, Your Beauty, Your Self.* New York: Fairchild Publications, 1994.

Mathis, Darlene, and Carole Jackson. *Women of Color, the Multicultural Guide to Fashion and Beauty.* SPCK and Triangle, 1999.

McJimsey, H.T. *Art in Clothing Selection.* New York: Harper and Row, 1963.

Miller-Lewis, S. Jill. *Dressing Successfully.* Detroit, MI: Miller Design Studio, 1985.

Molloy, John T. *The New Woman's Dress for Success Book.* New York: Warner Books, Inc., 1996.

Morana, V. *The Parisian Woman's Guide to Style.* New York: Universe, 1999.

Nicholson, Joanne. *Dressing Smart in the New Millennium.* Manassas Park, VA: Impact Publications, 2000.

Nicholson, Joanne, and Judy Lewis-Crum. *Color Wonderful.* New York: Fantom Books, 1986.

Olds, Ruthanne. *Big & Beautiful: Become the Beautiful Person You Were Meant to Be.* Washington, DC: Acropolis Books Ltd., 1982.

Orbach, Susie. *Fat is a Feminist Issue . . . the Anti-diet Guide to Permanent Weight Loss.* New York: Paddington Press, 1978.

Patterson, Barbara, Nancy Meadows, and Carol Holcomb Dreger. *The Successful Woman.* Englewood Cliffs, NJ: Prentice-Hall, Inc. 1982.

Pooser, Doris. *Always in Style: Body Line, Proportion, and Color.* Washington, DC: Acropolis Books Ltd., 1986.

Proctor, Jane. *Clothes Sense: Dressing Your Best for Your Figure and Your Lifestyle.* New York: Doubleday & Co. Inc., 1985.

Rasband, Judith. *Wardrobe Strategies for Women.* New York: Fairchild Publications, 1996.

Schrader, Constance. *Nine to Five: The Complete Looks, Clothes, and Personality Handbook for the Working Woman.* Englewood Cliffs, NJ: Prentice-Hall, 1981.

Shea, Sandra J., and Mary Todd Lyon. *A Girl's Guide to Executive Success.* Berkeley, CA: Ten Speed Press, 1984.

Spillane, Mary, and Christine Sherlock. *Color Me Beautiful's Looking your Best: Color, Makeup, and Style.* Madison Books, 2002.

Straley, Carole. *Sensational Scarves: 44 Ways to Turn a Scarf into a Fabulous Fashion Look.* New York: Crown Publishers Inc., 1985.

Thompson, Jacqueline. *Image Impact: The Aspiring Woman's Personal Packaging Program.* New York: A.W. Publishers, Inc., 1981.

Wallace, JoAnne. *Dress With Style.* Old Tappan, New Jersey: Revell, 1983.

Wallach, Janet. *Looks That Work: How to Match Your Wardrobe to Your Professional Profile and Create the Image That is Right for You.* New York: Viking Press, 1986.

Wallach, Janet. *Working Wardrobe: Affordable Clothes That Work for You.* Washington, D.C.: Acropolis Books Ltd., 1981; New York: Warner Books, Inc., 1982.

Zeldis, Yona. *Coping With Beauty, Fitness, and Fashion.* New York: Rosen Group, 1987.

men and women

Aslett, Don. *Clutters Last Stand: Its Time to Dejunk Your Life.* Cincinnati, OH: Writers Digest, 1984.

Bailey, Covert. *Fit or Fat?* Boston, MA: Houghton, Mifflin Co., 1978.

Baker, Caroline. *The Benetton Color Style File.* New York: Viking Press, 1987.

Baldrige, Letitia. *Letitia Baldrige's New Complete Guide to Executive Manners.* New York: Scribner, 1985.

Bauml, Betty J., and Franz H. Bauml. *A Dictionary of Gestures.* Meuchen, NJ: Scarecrow Press Inc., 1975.

Bixler, Susan and Lisa Scherrer Dugan. *5 Steps to Professional Presence: How to Project Confidence, Competence, and Credibility at Work.* Adams Media Corporation, 2000.

Bixler, Susan, and Nancy Nix-Rice. *The New Professional Image: From Business Casual to the Ultimate Power Look.* Adams Media, 1997.

Bonnell, Kimberly. *What to Wear: A Style Handbook.* New York: St. Martin's, 1999.

Calasibetta, Charlotte Mankey. *Essential Terms of Fashion: A Collection of Definitions.* New York: Fairchild Publications, 1986.

Calasibetta, Charlotte Mankey, and Phyllis G. Tortora. *The Fairchild Dictionary of Fashion,* 3rd ed. New York: Fairchild Publications, 2003.

Carnegie, Dale. *How to Win Friends & Influence People*. New York: Simon & Schuster Inc., 1936.

Davis, Flora. *Inside Intuition*. New York: The New American Library, Inc., 1981.

Eiseman, Leatrice. *Alive With Color: The Total Color System for Women and Men*. Washington, DC: Acropolis Books Ltd., 1983.

Eisenberg, Abne M., and Ralph R. Smith, Jr. *Nonverbal Communication*. Indianapolis: The Bobbs-Merrill Company, Inc. 1971.

Elsea, Janet. *The Four-Minute Sell*. New York: Simon & Schuster, 1984.

Evatt, Crislynne. *How to Organize Your Closet . . . and Your Life*. New York: Ballantine Books, 1981.

Fast, Julius. *The Body Language of Sex, Power, and Aggression*. New York: M. Evans and Co., Inc., 1977.

Fast, Julius. *Body Language*. New York: M. Evans and Co. Inc., 1970.

Fekkai, Frédéric. *A Year of Style*. New York: Clarkson Potter, 2000.

Ford, Charlotte. *Book of Modern Manners*. New York: Simon & Schuster, 1980.

Gross, Kim Johnson, Jeff Stone, and Linda Gillan Griffin. *What Should I Wear? Dressing for Occasions*. New York: Alfred A. Knopf, 1998.

Gross, Kim Johnson and Jeff Stone. *Work Clothes: Casual Dress for Serious Work*. New York: Knopf, 1996.

Harrison, Randall P. *Beyond Words*. Englewood Cliffs, NJ: Prentice-Hall, Inc., 1974.

Hayakawa, S.I. *Language in Thought & Action*. San Diego, CA: Harcourt Brace Jovanovich Inc., 1978.

Hix, Charles. *How to Dress Your Man*. New York: Crown Publishers, Inc., 1981.

Hoffman, Adeline M. *Clothing for the Handicapped, the Aged, and Other People with Special Needs*. Springfield, IL: C.C. Thomas, 1979.

Horn, Marilyn J., and Lois M. Gurel. *The Second Skin: An Interdisciplinary Study of Clothing*, 3rd ed. Boston, MA: Houghton Mifflin Co., 1981.

Kaiser, Susan B. *The Social Psychology of Clothing and Personal Adornment*. New York: MacMillan Publishing Company, 1985.

Knapp, Mark L. *Nonverbal Communication in Human Interaction*. New York: Holt, Rinehart and Winston, Inc., 1972.

Lavington, Camille and Stephanie Losee. *You've Only Got Three Seconds: How to Make the Right Impression in your Business and Social Life*. Doubleday, 1997.

Lee, Michelle. *Fashion Victim, Our Love-Hate Relationship with Dressing, Shopping, and the Cost of Style*. Broadway, 2003.

Lurie, Alison. *The Language of Clothes*. New York: Random House Inc., 1981.

Luscher, Dr. Max. *The Luscher Color Test*. New York: Washington Square Press, 1969.

Maysonave, Sherry. *Casual Power: How to Power Up Your Nonverbal Communication and Dress Down for Success*. Bright Books Inc, 1999.

Mazzei, George. *The New Office Etiquette: A Guide to Getting Along in the Corporate Age*. New York: Poseidon Press, 1983.

Mehrabian, Albert. *Silent Messages*. Belmont, CA: Wadsworth Publishing Co., Inc., 1971.

Morris, Desmond. *Manwatching: A Field Guide to Human Behavior*. New York: Harry N. Abrams, Inc., 1977.

Morrison, Tricia, Kyle Henderson, and Robert Woods. *No Mother, No Mirror: A Guide to Gaining a Personal Edge With Business*. Houghton Mifflin, June, 2000.

Nierenberg, Gerald I., and Henry H. Calero. *How to Read a Person Like a Book*. New York: Pocket Books, 1971.

Payne, Richard A. *Market Yourself for Success*. Englewood Cliffs, NJ: Prentice-Hall, 1984.

Pease, Allan. *Signals: How to Use Body Language for Power, Success, and Love*. New York: Bantam Books, 1984.

Post, Peggy, and Peter Post. *The Etiquette Advantage in Business*. Harper Resource Publication, 1999.

Ries, Al, and Jack Trout. *Positioning: The Battle for Your Mind*. New York: McGraw-Hill, Inc., 1981.

Robinson, Katherine. *The Clothing Care Handbook*. New York: Fawcett Books, 1985.

Sarnoff, Dorothy. *Speech Can Change Your Life*. New York: Hill & Wang, Inc., 1960.

Stamper, Anita A., Sue Humphries Sharp, and Linda B. Donnell. *Evaluating Apparel Quality*. New York: Fairchild Publications, 1991.

Storm, Penny. *Functions of Dress: Tool of Culture and the Individual*. Englewood Cliffs, NJ: Prentice-Hall, 1987.

Tortora, Phyllis G. *The Fairchild Encyclopedia of Fashion Accessories*. New York: Fairchild Publications, 2003.

Vanderbilt, Amy. *Amy Vanderbilt's Everyday Etiquette*. New York: Bantam Books, 1980.

Vanderbilt, Amy. *Etiquette*. New York: Doubleday, 1972.

Vermes, Jean C. *Complete Book of Business Etiquette*. Englewood Cliffs, NJ: Parker Publishing Co., Inc., 1976.

Zunin, Leonard. *Contact: The First Four Minutes*. New York: Ballantine Books, 1982.

about the authors

anne fenner

Anne Fenner is owner of Anne Fenner, Image Management, a professional image consulting firm she founded in 1981. Through presentations, consultations, and wardrobe acquisitions, her firm advises men, women, and companies on their images. She is a Phi Beta Kappa graduate of the University of Kansas and has a master's degree in arts and teaching from Northwestern University. Anne moved to Omaha in 1972 from Washington, D.C.

Anne likes helping people take charge of their lives by helping them with their image. She is committed to truth and beauty, and she perceives beauty to be much deeper than the physical.

sandi bruns

Sandi Bruns is owner of Bruns Graphics, a commercial art and design studio specializing in the creation of unique and personal visual and verbal statements for companies and individuals. She is a graduate of the University of Iowa where she majored in Home Economics, specializing in clothing, textiles, and design. She is a member of Phi Upsilon Omicron and Alpha Lambda Delta honoraries. Sandi holds a master's of fine arts degree from the University of Hawaii. She moved to Omaha from San Francisco in 1972.

Sandi enjoys being a part of the creative energy of the universe and is glad that we all have the opportunity to be part of that process. She finds that the world can often be a very funny place . . . especially the people.

index